Susan L. Lingo

COLLECT-N-TELL

BiBLE STORIES for Kids

Standard®
PUBLISHING
Bringing The Word to Life

Cincinnati, Ohio

Dedication

"We give thanks to you, O God,
we give thanks, for your Name is near;
men tell of your wonderful deeds."

Collect-n-Tell Bible Stories for Kids
Copyright © 2002 Susan L. Lingo

Published by Standard Publishing, Cincinnati, Ohio
www.standardpub.com

Credits
Produced by Susan L. Lingo, Bright Ideas Books™
Cover design by Diana Walters
Illustrated by Marilynn G. Barr and Paula Becker

11 10 09 08   8 7 6 5 4
ISBN-13: 978-0-7847-1418-8
ISBN-10: 0-7847-1418-5

CONTENTS

OLD TESTAMENT

NEW TESTAMENT

NOW, ENGAGING BIBLE-STORY LESSONS ARE AS SIMPLE AS 1-2-3 WITH

Collect-n-Tell Bible Stories for Kids!

Get ready to present oodles of exciting, life-changing Bible stories with powerful biblical messages—in just three easy steps. First, collect a variety of everyday items. Next, place them in a bag, box, or basket along with this copy of *Collect-n-Tell Bible Stories for Kids.* Now you're ready to present engaging Bible stories through super storytelling techniques. But don't be fooled! These are Bible stories and presentations that truly get God's Word across in memorable ways that engage kids' minds, hearts, and bodies. You might call it fun with a focus! And with the handy Story Kit and book at hand, you can present these super story times with a minimum of preparation and practice. *Collect-n-tell Bible Stories for Kids* provides thirty-four life-changing Bible stories, including seven Wow 'Em Bible stories that require a few extra items but are guaranteed to grab even the most fleeting of attention spans! Simply follow these directions for assembling your very own Story Kit in a snap! (Directions for preparing the special Story Apron and Picture Props are included at the end of this introduction.)

COLLECT EVERYDAY ITEMS. Check your garage, kitchen, or attic for the list of everyday items on page 7. Check off the items as they're collected. You may wish to photocopy the list and place it in a spot where church members can see what's needed and donate the items over a week or two. Be sure to place a decorated box below the list to handle the collections. (Your kids might even wish to make an announcement to the entire church explaining what they're collecting and inviting the congregation to help out.) If enough extra items are contributed, consider making a second kit and purchasing another copy of *Collect-n-Tell Bible Stories for Kids* to add to the kit. Present your super service project to another class at church, a Christian school, or a daycare center. What a great way to get God's Word to others in a fun way!

(Note: You will also need standard classroom supplies such as crayons and markers, scissors, glue, clear tape, white copy paper, pencils. These items are not included in your Story Kit list, but feel free to add them to the kit if it would make your preparation easier!)

PLACE ITEMS IN A BAG, BOX, OR BASKET. Let kids help decorate a box with a lid to hold your collected Story Kit items. Colorful self-adhesive paper, gift wrap, or even rolled adhesive cork work well. (Remember, you'll want something sturdy to last for years of learning fun!) Or consider using a large mesh bag that normally holds laundry or even a bright, plastic laundry basket as a kit to hold your Story Kit items. Don't forget to keep a copy of the Bible and *Collect-n-Tell Bible Stories for Kids* in your Story Kit!

GET SET TO TELL A SUPER STORY! That's all there is to it! You're now ready to present your kids with a super selection of Bible stories with storytelling techniques that are as memorable as they are filled with learning fun!

DIRECTIONS FOR THE STORY APRON AND PICTURE PROPS

Picture Props
1. Photocopy the illustrations from pages 110-112 on heavy stock paper, then color and cut out the pictures. (Kids love helping!)
2. Cover the pictures with clear, self-adhesive paper for durability.
3. Store the pictures in a large envelope labeled "Picture Props" and keep the envelope in your Story Kit.
(Consider making several copies of the pictures to use in craft projects, displays, or to let kids make their own Bible storytelling kits.)

Story Apron
1. Cut out seven 6-inch construction paper or fabric "pockets" and use permanent markers to number the pockets one through seven. (Fabric will be more durable!)
2. Use colorful vinyl or electrical tape to tape three sides of each pocket to a disposable or fabric apron. (Use fabric glue to glue fabric pockets to the apron.) Keep the Story Apron in your Story Kit.

STORY KIT ITEMS FOR
Collect-n-Tell Bible Stories for Kids

Collect the following items or sets of items and place them in a large bag, box, or basket to present loads of super Bible stories that powerfully teach God's truths. Check off the items as they're collected.

- ❏ Bible
- ❏ *Collect-n-Tell Bible Stories for Kids*
- ❏ paper plates
- ❏ a ball of string
- ❏ white shelf paper and newspapers
- ❏ permanent markers
- ❏ index cards
- ❏ a ball
- ❏ lunch sacks
- ❏ masking tape
- ❏ a package of balloons
- ❏ 10 hinge-style clothespins
- ❏ 3 men's neckties
- ❏ 5 plastic coins
- ❏ bolt of ribbon
- ❏ plastic spoons
- ❏ 3 white dish towels
- ❏ 1 large jingle bell
- ❏ 1 empty pop can
- ❏ plastic shower curtain
- ❏ cookie sheet
- ❏ **Story Apron (see page 6 for directions)**
- ❏ **Picture Props (see page 6 for directions)**

CREATION POWER!

Only God creates through his power and love.

Genesis 1:1-2:3; Psalm 100:3; Jeremiah 10:12

BEFORE BEGINNING...

Before beginning, gather the Story Kit items as well as the following classroom supplies: markers, scissors, and paper. Cut out a 3-inch paper tree and draw a row of "Zzz's" on an index card. Make sure you've photocopied the appropriate Picture Props. Slide the picture of the sun into pocket #1, the tree into pocket #3, the star into pocket #4, the fish into pocket #5, the pictures of the man and woman and donkey into pocket #6, and the "Zzz's" into pocket #7. Pocket #2 will be empty to represent "air." Set aside the ball. You'll be reading a poem that lists the days of creation and what God made each day as you pull the accompanying pictures from the Story Apron. Kids will discover that only God can create through his awesome power and love.

Story Kit Supplies

- ❑ Bible
- ❑ Story Apron
- ❑ ball
- ❑ 1 index card
- ❑ Picture Props (man, woman, donkey, fish, star, sun)

TELLING THE STORY

Tie the Story Apron around your waist or the waist of a child. Gather kids in a group and ask:

★ *When was a time you made something, such as a craft or food item?*
★ *What materials or ingredients did you use to make your special something?*

Say: **We make lots of pretty and useful things such as get-well cards for sick friends or yummy recipes or special craft projects. We need materials and different ingredients anytime we make something, but there is someone who can create things from nothing at all! We can make things only by using materials that God has already created, but only God is our Creator. And only God can create from nothing through his power and love. Let's** listen to a story rhyme about the time God created the world and all that is in it and above it. We'll pretend this ball represents the world. See if you can remember the order in which God created everything. Hold up a finger each time you hear on what day God created something special and say, "God saw that it was good!"

Read the following story rhyme, revealing pictures from the Story Apron pockets when directed. Lead kids in counting the days of creation on their fingers. Repeat two times, inviting children to name the things in creation as they're revealed.

> *In the beginning, God created the sky and the earth in his powerful, loving way,* (toss the ball to someone and have it tossed back to you)
> *But what were the things God created each and every day?*
> *Day 1—let there be light;* (pocket #1—reveal the sun)
> *Day 2—the air so bright!* (pocket #2—"toss" a pretend handful of air from the pocket upward)
> *Day 3—land, seas, and plants;* (pocket #3—reveal the tree)
> *Day 4—the sky-lights dance!* (pocket #4—reveal the star)
> *Day 5—swimmy fish and birds that flew,* (pocket #5—reveal the fish)
> *Day 6—and animals and people, too!* (pocket #6—reveal the donkey, man, and woman)
> *Day 7—was God's special day of rest.* (pocket #7—reveal the "Zzz" card)
> *And this is how the world was blessed!* (Toss the ball to each child and have him say, "Thank you, God!," then toss the ball back.)

Say: **Wow! The Bible tells us that in seven days, God created all the world and all that's above it and on it. And God made each part of his creation with love, imagination, and care. He put colorful petals on flowers and provided different kinds of clouds for us to enjoy. And God made delicious foods to taste, sounds to hear, and so many other things we love and delight in! Could we make trees and bees and bendable knees from nothing? No way! Only God can create from nothing through his power and love. Let's explore more about God's power to create by reading some verses in the Bible.**

MAKING IT MEMORABLE

Invite volunteers to read aloud Psalm 100:3 and Jeremiah 10:12, then ask:
> ★ *In what ways did God's creation show his wisdom? his love? his power?*

★ *How did God feel about his creation? In other words, did God see that it was good?*

★ *What is your favorite part of God's creation?*

★ *Who is the only true Creator?*

Say: **We've learned that God created the world and all that is in it and above it and on it, and he saw that it was good. But God didn't stop creating with people and nature! He made something else that's wonderful and warm. Let's see what else God created.** Read aloud 1 John 4:19, then say: **God created love! And we love because God first loved us! God made all the beautiful things in the world and the heavens, and he also made love to share with creation. What an awesome God we serve! Let's share a prayer of thanks for all God has made and for being the only true Creator.**

After praying, have kids repeat this short action rhyme two times to remind them of all God has made. Then if there's time, close by singing "He's Got the Whole World in His Hands."

> **God is our Creator—as mighty as can be.** *(point upward, then make muscles)*
>
> **God made the earth and animals;** *(make a circle with your arms, then make rabbit ears)*
>
> **The sky, the seas, and—me!** *(put hands overhead, make hand waves, point to yourself)*

Play a lively game of Creation Toss using the ball. Have kids form a circle, then toss the ball back and forth across the circle as they name favorite parts of God's creation. Older kids will enjoy the challenge of tossing the ball and naming the order in which God created the world. Keep repeating the order until all kids have had at least one turn to name a day of creation.

NOAH SAYS GRACE

God showed his grace in the toughest of times!

Genesis 6:9-8:21; 9:13-17; 2 Corinthians 9:8; Ephesians 2:8

BEFORE BEGINNING...

Before beginning, gather the Story Kit items as well as the following classroom supplies: white copy paper or tissue paper, scissors, and markers. Cut a paper plate in half and use markers to color a rainbow on that half. You'll also need to color a whole paper plate yellow for the sun. Kids will use the Story Kit items to tell the story of Noah and the ark. There should be a part for every child to play. If you have a large class, let extra kids play plastic spoons for the raindrops or have more than a few kids swish copy paper or tissue paper for the rustling of wind. The empty pop can will provide the sounds of animal hooves clip-clopping up to the ark as will the jingle bell (for cows, goats, and sheep). Use an 8-foot length of ribbon for two kids to make waves, and have a child be the "sun" and one the "rainbow" as they hold up the colored paper plates. Finally, two or more kids can hold up the top edge of the shower curtain to make the ark. (You may need to adjust the number of items to the size of your class to retell the story.)

Story Kit Supplies

❑ Bible
❑ shower curtain
❑ empty pop can
❑ ribbon
❑ paper plates
❑ jingle bell
❑ 1 necktie
❑ 1 dish towel
❑ plastic spoons

TELLING THE STORY

Set the Story Kit items and other props on the floor. Then gather kids around the items and invite them to tell about times that were very hard, frustrating, or scary and how they made it through those tough times. Then say: **We all face trying times or days that feel dark and even scary. It's so good to know that God's grace and help shine brightly in the toughest of times! Let's retell a story of God's grace and how he helped Noah get through the darkest and stormiest time and how Noah discovered the power of God's good grace. You can all help tell this exciting story.**

Invite a child to play Noah and have him drape the dish towel around his head and secure it by tying the necktie as a headband. Then choose two or more kids to hold up the shower-curtain ark at the appropriate time. Hand out the pop can and jingle bell to kids being animals coming to the ark. Give the paper-plate sun and rainbow to two kids to hold up at the appropriate times. You'll need two volunteers to hold the ribbon in front of the ark and make waves at the proper time. The remainder of the kids can rustle copy paper or tissue paper for sounds of "wind" and "waves," and others can tap plastic spoons in the rhythm of falling rain.

Read or retell the story of Noah and the ark from Genesis 6:9-8:21. Tell how God told Noah to build an ark (have kids holding the shower curtain raise it little by little to the pounding kids make on the floor with their fists). Explain how God sent the animals to the ark as the kids playing the parts of animals clomp the can and jingle the bell as they march up to stand behind the lifted shower-curtain ark. Recount how the storms came just as God promised and invite kids holding papers and plastic spoons to rustle and tap their items to make the sounds of wind and rain. Remind kids that Noah and the inhabitants of the ark sailed for many days and nights and trusted in God's good grace and love to protect them and provide for them.

Then tell how God sent the wind and sun to dry the land. Have kids rustle their papers and position the child holding the paper-plate sun beside the ark. Explain that God, through his grace and love, put the first rainbow in the sky as his promise never to destroy the earth again by flood. Have the child holding the rainbow plate stand on the other side of the ark from the sun. Remind kids that when Noah left the ark, the first thing he did was thank God for his amazing grace. Invite everyone to leave the ark and march to stand in front as they shout, "Thank you, God, for your great grace!"

Set aside the Story Kit items and say: **That was wonderful! What a powerful story of God's grace, protection, and love! God's grace was great when he chose to save Noah, his family, and the animals. And his grace was great when he gave his promise to Noah and us never to destroy the world by flooding it again. Now let's discover how Noah said a special prayer thanking God for his great grace.**

MAKING IT MEMORABLE

Invite volunteers to read aloud Genesis 9:13-17; 2 Corinthians 9:8; and Ephesians 2:8. Then ask:

★ *What did Noah do when God led everyone from the ark?*
★ *Why did Noah want to thank God?*
★ *In what ways did God show his grace to Noah, his family, and the animals on the ark?*
★ *How does God show his grace to us?*

Say: **Noah faced a scary time, didn't he? He had a huge boat to build with his bare hands and only the help of his family. He had to care for his family and all the animals on the ark. And Noah didn't know where or when or even if the waters would go down. But God showed his love and grace by protecting, loving, and honoring the obedience of Noah and those on the ark. And God has shown his grace to us as well by promising never to destroy the world again through floods. God demonstrates his love and grace to us in so many ways, and just like Noah, we can thank God for his grace.**

Spread the shower-curtain ark on the floor and invite kids to gather "aboard." Join hands and pray: **Dear God, we thank you for helping us through hard times by your loving grace. Help us trust you as Noah did, and remind our hearts to ask for your help and grace in times that are tough. Amen.** End by singing "Amazing Grace" or "Arky, Arky."

Let kids make cool Grace-Mat place mats. Use permanent markers or paint pens to decorate vinyl place mats, or make construction-paper arks covered in clear self-adhesive paper. Use permanent markers to write: "God's grace is great!" on one side of the mats, then have kids each write a thank-you "grace" to God on the other side. Challenge kids to share their special prayers of grace at mealtime with their families.

TOWER OF PRIDE

Our all-powerful God wants us to be humble.

Genesis 11:1-9; Proverbs 3:34; 11:2; 16:18; 29:23

BEFORE BEGINNING...

Story Kit Supplies

❑ **Bible**
❑ **index cards**
❑ **jingle bell**
❑ **white shelf paper**

Before beginning, gather the Story Kit items as well as the following classroom supplies: scissors, markers, and tape. Cut a 2-foot piece of white shelf paper and write the following two lines on it: "Build up pride, and it will tear you down— / But a humble spirit makes grace abound!" Tape the paper to a wall or door where kids can see it. Be sure you have plenty of index cards, since kids will be constructing card towers. Two teams of kids will build the tallest towers they can. After they add every five cards (four "walls" and a "roof"), one team member must run to the opposite end of the room and ring the jingle bell, then rush back to add more cards. After five minutes, you'll call time and see how well the building went and what happened to the towers when they became too tall. Kids will listen to the Bible story about the tower of Babel as they discover what negative things pride can do and why God desires us to be humble and know that he alone is God.

TELLING THE STORY

Form two teams at one end of the room and hand each team thirty index cards to start. (If teams need more cards, be ready to supply them.) Place the jingle bell on the floor at the opposite end of the room. Explain that you'll kick off your Bible-story time with a quick-paced race. Tell kids they'll be building tall towers using the index cards. Show kids how to make four walls using the cards, then add a card roof. Tell kids that each time five cards are used and another story is added to the tower, one team member must rush to the jingle bell and ring it. Then team members are to add another story on top of the first and so on. Tell kids they'll have five minutes to build. If a tower tumbles at any time, they must begin to rebuild the tower from scratch.

When five minutes is up, call time and look at the towers. Point out how difficult it was to keep the towers standing. Ask:

★ *Why wasn't it as easy to build the towers as it sounded?*

★ *How did pride make you rush to try to build the biggest and best tower?*

★ *What do you think the saying "Pride goes before a fall" means?*

Say: **When you began this race to build a tower, you might have thought, "This is easy. I'm the best at building like this!" or maybe you just knew your team would build a bigger and better tower than the other team. But what happened? Towers tumbled, time ran out, and you discovered that a tower to the ceiling just couldn't be accomplished! Long ago in Old Testament times, the people in a certain place felt the same way. They were filled with empty pride and decided to build a tower all the way to God. They wanted to be like him and to rule in the heavens. But their pride caused them great destruction and a mighty fall. Let's hear the story of the Tower of Babel. Each time you hear the word "pride," repeat the first line of this rhyme.** Show kids the paper taped to the wall and read aloud the first line: "Build up pride, and it will tear you down." **And when you hear the word "humble," repeat the second line.** Read aloud the second line of the rhyme: "But a humble spirit makes grace abound!"

Long ago, people all had one language and one speech. When the people came together, they thought how great it would be if they could work together to build a huge city with a tower that could reach all the way to heaven. "Then we'll really be special!" they thought. But their *pride* was showing! Those people had such *pride* that they thought they could be like God. They weren't being *humble* at all and forgot to remember that there's only one God. After all, they thought, if we can make a tower to heaven, then we'll be just like God, right?

Wrong! Their foolish *pride* took over, and the people began building that awful tower. Up and up it went—up, that is, until God saw what they were doing. God was angry that the people had such *pride*—especially when God desires us to have *humble* spirits and attitudes. So God tumbled that tower and scattered the people all over the world. And he mixed up their languages so they could no longer do such *prideful*—and destructive—planning. And that is why the tower was called "Babel," because it was there that God confused the language of the whole world because of the foolish *pride* that had consumed it.

Say: **Whoa! God was very angry at the people's pride and ego, wasn't he? Those people were very foolish in thinking that they could become like God. Their pride got the better of them. God desires us to have a humble spirit and to admit and know that there is only one all-powerful God. Let's explore more about why having a prideful attitude is foolish and why being humble and giving God the glory is wise.**

MAKING IT MEMORABLE

Form four groups and assign each group one of the following verses to read from Proverbs: 3:34; 11:2; 16:18; and 29:23. Have kids discuss in their groups what the verses teach us about pride and humility. Then invite each group to read its verse aloud and share their thoughts about what it is teaching. When each group has had a turn, ask:

★ *Why is being too proud and filled with ego a bad thing?*
★ *How does pride hurt our relationship with God?*
★ *Why does God prefer a humble spirit over haughtiness and pride?*
★ *Why is it important as well as wise to admit that God is all-powerful and the only God we worship?*

Say: **Remember the saying I asked you about earlier, "Pride goes before a fall"? That familiar saying comes right from God's Word.** Read aloud Proverbs 16:18 once more, then say: **God teaches us that being haughty and prideful causes us to do foolish things and may cause our self-destruction and fall—just as it did when sin entered the world in the Garden of Eden! Pride caused Adam and Eve to want to be like God, and what happened? They fell from God's grace and were tossed out of the garden. God still loved them, but he hated the pride! And just like the people of Babel whose pride caused them to fall, pride can cause our downfall, too, if we're not careful. Let's pray and ask God to help us always have a spirit of humility and to acknowledge that he alone is God and can do all things.**

Share a prayer, then sing, "Awesome God" if there's time.

Let kids draw a tall tower on 6-foot-long pieces of white shelf paper. Color in the bricks on the tower using brown crayons or cut "bricks" from the lunch sacks in the Story Kit and glue them on the tower. Write the following rhyme on the poster: "Build up pride, and it will tear you down—But a humble spirit makes grace abound!" Then add Proverbs 3:34 along the bottom of the poster. Challenge kids to hang their posters in their rooms and ask God each day to keep them humble and to help them give God the credit for every good thing they do.

FOLLOW THE LEADER

We can trust God to lead us in our every move.

Genesis 11:27-12:9; Psalms 31:14; 91:2; Proverbs 3:5, 6

BEFORE BEGINNING...

Before beginning, gather the Story Kit items as well as the following classroom supplies: markers and white copy paper. Before class, place a winding path on the floor using masking tape. Make the pathway begin at one end of the room and wind to the opposite end. In this story lesson, kids will discover that, like Abram, we can learn about God's character by seeing how he acts toward us, and in this way we learn to trust him and his plans for us.

Story Kit Supplies

❏ Bible
❏ 1 kit item for each child
❏ masking tape

TELLING THE STORY

Place the Story Kit items in a pile and invite kids to choose items that they like or that interest them. Then have kids sit in a large circle. Say: **We can tell a lot about people by what they like, dislike, how they act, and the words they say. Let's go around the circle and give each of you a turn to tell something about yourself using the item you chose.** Encourage kids to tell their name and age and why they chose the item they chose. Then ask:

★ *Why is it good to learn things about others?*
★ *In what ways do people's actions tell about them?*

Say: **We know lots of things about lots of people. But what do you know about God? What is he really like, and can we truly trust God? Reading Bible stories helps us learn more about God and his character, and the story of how Abram trusted God when God called him to move to a new home teaches us a lot about the trustworthiness of God. Moving days can really tell a lot about people and their character! We can see how willing people are to move and how well they trust the reasons for moving to new homes. We can see how hard they work, how patient they are with others, and how easily discouraged they might become. Let's join Abram in the**

story about his big move and how he discovered a lot about trusting God and his character. As we listen to the story, you can move along this pathway and haul your Story Kit item along. The first way you'll haul your items is . . . on your head!

Tell the following story and have kids move at the appropriate times and in the ways specified. Begin at one end of the room and move, bit by bit, down the tape path to the opposite end of the room.

Abram was a man who loved God and wanted to obey him. Now Abram lived in a comfy house in the city of Ur with his wife Sarai. Abram was comfortable in his house, so when God called Abram one day and told Abram to follow him, Abram probably was a bit nervous! But God had promised Abram a new home in a wonderful promised land God would lead them to. So Abram packed his belongings and family and began to move. Walk five steps along the path carrying your items on your head. Pause for kids to begin their "moving day" travels, then continue: **Sarai wondered where they were going—so did Abram. Many people wouldn't have followed God without travel plans or maps or a final destination in sight. But because Abram loved and trusted God, he kept following. Take five more steps along the pathway as you balance your items on your palms.** Again, wait for kids to move, then say: **Wow! Think of the trust it took to blindly follow God away from a cozy house into the unknown. Why do you think Abram followed God?** Let kids share their ideas, then continue: **God kept Abram and his family safe on their journey, and that helped Abram trust God. God spoke to Abram and Abram prayed to God, and that helped Abram trust God. And Abram knew God was all-powerful and loving, and that kept his trust moving along. Walk along the pathway ten more steps balancing your moving packs on your shoulders.**

After kids have moved again, say: **God promised Abram he would lead him to a new land, and Abram trusted that God always keeps his promises. And so on and on they all went, step by step, move by move, until God told them to stop! Walk to the end of the pathway this time on your hands and knees with your items on your backs.**

When kids have made it to the end of the tape path, have them sit in place and hold their items. Say: **God had led Abram and his family to a new place called Canaan, and it was here that God gave Abram another special promise. God promised Abram that he would have as many children as there are stars in the sky! Do you think that promise came true?** Allow kids time to answer and explain their thoughts. Then say: **Abram became the father of many nations because he trusted God and learned that God is loving, powerful, protective, and totally trustworthy! Toss your items in the air and shout, "Trust God in your every move!"** Pause. **Now let's discover more about God's character and how we can learn to trust and follow him just as Abram did.** Place the Story Kit items aside.

MAKING IT MEMORABLE

Form four groups and give each group a sheet of paper and marker. Assign each group one of the following verses from Psalms to read and discuss: 31:14; 52:8; 56:4; and 91:2. Have groups list what they discover about God and how we can trust him from their verses. Then have each group read aloud its verse and share what they learned about trust. Ask:

★ *What did you learn about God from the story of Abram's big move?*
★ *Can we trust God just as Abram did? Explain.*
★ *In what ways does trusting God demonstrate our love for him?*
★ *How can you trust God more this week?*

Read Proverbs 3:5, 6, then say: **Through learning about they way God treats us and the people we read of in the Bible, we discover many things about what God is really like. God kept his promises to Abram, so Abram trusted him. God kept Abram and his family safe on their journey, so we know God protects us. And God led Abram to a wonderful new place, and that showed God's love and care. When we take the time to learn about God and the wonderful things he does, it's easy to put our trust in him! Let's end with a prayer thanking God for his faithfulness.** Share a prayer, then close by singing "Father Abraham" if there's time.

Play a lively game using the ball from the Story Kit. Have kids scatter around the room and take turns tossing the ball to one another. Each time someone catches the ball, have that child tell one character trait of God, such as "faithfulness," "trust," "love," or "keeps his promises." Continue until everyone has had a turn to name two character traits of God.

THE BIG SWITCH

We want to treasure the blessings God gives us.

Genesis 25:29-34; Proverbs 15:6; Matthew 7:6

BEFORE BEGINNING...

Story Kit Supplies

❑ Bible
❑ 3 lunch sacks

Before beginning, gather the Story Kit items. Since this is a Wow 'Em Bible story, you'll also need a penny and a nickel for each child and a treat for each child, such as a key chain, magnet, fancy gel pen, or pencil. Place the pennies, nickels, and treats in three lunch sacks, one group per sack. In this Bible story about the time Esau traded his birthright to Jacob, kids will be choosing whether to make their own trades or be happy with what they have. Kids will each receive a penny to begin the lesson. During the Bible story when Esau chooses to trade his father's blessing and birthright for a bowl of stew, kids can decide whether to keep their pennies or trade them for something deemed more valuable: nickels. Most kids will probably trade, but will discover later that the pennies were worth much more! This Bible-story lesson will help kids realize that the treasures God gives us shouldn't be tossed away and that there may be bad consequences when we do so.

TELLING THE STORY

Place the sack containing the treats in a hidden place. Set the penny and nickel lunch sacks beside you and have kids sit in a circle on the floor. (Keep track of which sack is which.) Shake the penny sack and say: **In this sack there is a treasure for each one of you that is worth much. What do you think is in this sack?** Allow time for kids to share their ideas, then hand out the pennies, one to a child. Say: **Do you think this is a great treasure worth much? Well later you will have a choice to make. You can keep your penny or trade it for a nickel!** Dump the nickels out of the bag in the center of the circle. **Our Bible story today is about a man named Esau who had to choose between keeping what was his by birth or trading it for something he thought was** more valuable. **When we get to the place in the story when Esau makes his choice, you will be able to choose what to do, too.**

Retell the story of how Esau traded his birthright to his brother Jacob for a bowl of stew from Genesis 25:29-34. Say: **There were two brothers, named Esau and Jacob. They were twins, but Esau was a bit older because he had been born first. Long ago, the firstborn son received not only a special blessing from his father but also most of the family treasures as well. This was called a "birthright," and it was greatly treasured. Esau was the first-born son, so the birthright was his—but it was something Jacob wanted very much. One day Jacob was cooking a delicious pot of stew when his older brother came in from working hard. "I'm so hungry!" said Esau. "Give me some of that wonderful stew!" Jacob said, "I will—if you sell me your birthright. Trade me this stew for your birthright!" Esau had a choice.** Pause, then say: **And so do you!** Have kids decide if they will trade their pennies in for nickels. Make a pile of pennies in the center of the circle for kids who choose to trade their pennies in.

When everyone has made a choice, continue with the story: **Esau had a choice. He was *so* hungry right that very minute! And what good would a birthright be in years to come if he couldn't eat now? Besides, he didn't care for his birthright—he thought it wasn't worth anything. So Esau traded his blessing and birthright for a bowl of stew! Years later, Esau would wish he hadn't done this, and he learned that God gives us things of value that are to be treasured, not tossed aside. And so God blessed Jacob, and he became the father of the nation of Israel!**

Say: **Wow! Esau traded off what he thought wasn't worth anything—but it certainly was! Now let's see what trades you might have made.**

MAKING IT MEMORABLE

Have kids hold up their coins, then ask:
★ *Did you choose to trade? Why or why not?*
★ *What makes one thing seem more valuable than another?*
★ *Do we always see the value in God's blessings all at once? Explain.*

Say: **Esau didn't realize the value of his blessing and birthright when he was hungry. He was too driven by what he wanted at that moment in time. But when God gives us something or provides for us, we want to treasure it! Let's see what the Bible says about treasuring what is ours with God.**

Read aloud Proverbs 15:6a and Matthew 7:6. Then say: **God's Word teaches us that God has many treasures in store for us when we are faithful and love him. And when we are given treasures and are blessed, we should not throw those blessings away—or we may be in big trouble later! We want to**

21

hold on to what God has given with all we are and thank him for all he has given as well! Now, who kept the pennies they had at first? They were the truly best treasure!

Hand kids who kept the pennies a treat from the treat sack. Say: **You saw the treasure in the pennies even when others didn't—just as Jacob saw the treasure in Esau's birthright when Esau didn't. But because all of you know the treasure we have in God's blessings now, you're all winners!** Hand out treats to the rest of the kids.

Share a prayer thanking God for his rich blessings and asking for his help always to hold on to all God has given us so we can use it to serve and love him better. If there's time, sing "Awesome God."

Let kids make Jacob's Stew to share with another class. Bring in cooked chicken or beef-stew pieces, cooked potatoes, and cooked carrots, peas, and celery. Have kids cut up the tender meat and cooked vegetables. Place the ingredients in an electric skillet and pour a can of stewed tomatoes over the stew. Heat the stew for ten minutes, then serve another class and enjoy sharing your treat as you remind them to treat God's blessings with care and appreciation.

RED SEA FAITH

Faith in God's ultimate power can save us.

Exodus 14:1-29; Ephesians 2:8; Hebrews 10:39

BEFORE BEGINNING...

Before beginning, gather the Story Kit items as well as the following classroom supplies: scissors, a stapler or tape, and markers. Cut two 3-foot lengths of ribbon and place them on the floor, parallel to each other and approximately 1 foot apart. The ribbons will form the make-believe "sea" you use during the story. As you retell the story of the Israelites' escape from Egypt, kids will leap across the ribbon sea as it grows wider with each leap. In this story lesson, kids will discover that Moses and the rest of God's people had to make a giant leap of faith as they followed God out of Egypt and across the roaring Red Sea. They'll also explore how we make leaps of faith to trust God's saving power. Kids will use index cards and cut ribbon to make bookmarks for the story of the Red Sea crossing in their Bibles.

Story Kit Supplies

- ❏ **Bible**
- ❏ **ribbon**
- ❏ **index cards**

TELLING THE STORY

Gather children on one side of the ribbons and explain that this is a pretend sea. Ask:
- ★ ***Did you ever wonder if God could help you when you had real troubles to overcome?***
- ★ ***How did you know God would be there to protect and help?***

Say: **The Bible tells us about a time Moses wondered those same things when he and God's people were in real trouble. You can help tell this amazing story about a wondrous escape made possible by God's perfect power. Whenever you hear me say, "a great leap of faith," leap across the sea and shout, "Only by God's great power!" Each time you make a leap of faith, the ribbon sea will grow a bit wider for the next leap.**

23

Tell the following story of the Israelites' escape from Pharaoh across the Red Sea from Exodus 14:1-29, signaling kids when it's time to leap across the ribbon sea and to shout victoriously. Each time kids leap across, move the ribbons a few inches apart.

For many, many years the Israelites had been slaves of the wicked Pharaoh of Egypt, who made God's people make bricks in the hot sun and haul them to make his temples. Oh, how the people wanted to be free! But it would be such *a great leap of faith* to trust God to free them! (Pause as kids leap, then widen the ribbons a bit.) Continue: **Would God hear their cries for help? Could God's power be great enough to save them? What *a great leap of faith* it would take.** (Pause as kids leap, then widen the ribbons a bit.)

But God did hear their cries for help and sent Moses to help free the people. God sent incredible disasters to Pharaoh to show his power—frogs and bugs and blisters and even death. But would God's powerful plan work? It would take *a great leap of faith* for the Israelites to believe they could be free! (Pause as kids leap, then widen the ribbons a bit more.)

But God's power is ultimate and perfect, and soon Pharaoh let Moses and God's people go free. They quickly left Egypt and traveled with God as their guide. But when they came to a great sea, they were afraid. Pharaoh's wicked soldiers were coming to get them, and they were trapped between the soldiers and the sea. It would take *a great leap of faith* to get out of this terrible mess! (Pause as kids leap, then widen the ribbons a bit more.)

But Moses and the Israelites kept their faith. And Moses prayed for God's great help. Then God told Moses to hold his walking stick over the water, and God parted the sea in half! God held the waters back while his people crossed safely to the other side. It was *a great leap of faith* and a parade of victory across that sea! (Pause as kids leap, then widen the ribbons a bit more.)

The wicked soldiers were drowned when God closed the waters, but the Israelites' faith in God's perfect power saved his people, and with *a great leap of faith* they praised and thanked God! Yeah! (Have kids leap across the ribbon, then leap in the air to praise God.)

Have kids sit on either side of the ribbon sea, then say: **What an exciting story of faith, trust, and God's glorious power to save us! Give each other high fives, then let's explore more about the power of faith and how God saves us by faith.**

MAKING IT MEMORABLE

Distribute the index cards and markers. Then invite volunteers to read aloud
Luke 7:50; Ephesians 2:8; and Hebrews 10:39. Ask:

★ *Why do you think God wants us to have faith in him?*

★ *How did faith in God save the Israelites? How can our faith save us?*

★ *In what ways does having faith in Jesus, God's perfect gift of love, save us?*

★ *What can you do to strengthen your faith in God?*

Say: **Faith in God and his power to save helped Moses lead the Israelites, and it helped the Israelites follow God. Our faith in God and in his Son Jesus can save us, too. Faith can help save us from sin and find our way out of troubles. And faith lifts our hearts and draws us closer to God. Let's make verse cards to help us learn a mighty verse about the power of faith!**

Have kids use markers to write Hebrews 10:39 on their index cards. Then cut 8-inch lengths of ribbon and staple or tape the ribbon to the index cards to make bookmarks. Challenge kids to read their bookmarks each day for the next week to memorize this verse about the power of faith. End with a prayer thanking God, as Moses did, for his power to save and help through our faith in him.

Sing "Awesome God" as you leap back and forth across the ribbon-streamer sea. After each leap, have kids name one way faith saves us. Young children might like to hop back and forth to the tune of "Ring Around the Rosie," but using these words:

Ring around the Red Sea—my faith in God will save me.
Splish-splash, splish-splash! Safe at last!

GOD'S TEN RULES

We express our love for God by obeying him.

Exodus 19:1, 2; 20:1-17; Deuteronomy 27:10; 28:1; 1 John 5:3

BEFORE BEGINNING...

Story Kit Supplies

- ❏ Bible
- ❏ ball of string
- ❏ 10 clothespins
- ❏ 10 index cards

Before beginning, gather the Story Kit items as well as the following classroom supplies: markers. Suspend a string clothesline across your room. Tie the ends of the string to two chairs, windows, or doorknobs. Place ten hinge-style clothespins below the clothesline. Write the ten commandments from this story on index cards, one commandment per card. (If you prefer, photocopy and cut apart the commandments on page 27 and glue each to a card.) Just prior to story time, place the index cards in a large circle. Kids will be stepping around the circle on the cards. After each commandment is read, you'll call "stop" and the child on or closest to the card with the commandment just read aloud will clip the card to the clothesline. This story-time lesson will be used to help kids identify reasons for rules and why God's rules are so important in keeping us safe, healthy, and happy.

TELLING THE STORY

Be sure the index cards are on the floor in a large circle and have kids stand in the circle. (Kids don't all have to be standing on a card.) Ask:

★ **What's an important rule you follow at home or in school?**

★ **Why are rules important to follow?**

Say: **Rules are made to keep us safe and happy. And rules are also made to show care and love. Parents and teachers make rules because they love you and want you to be safe and happy. God made special rules for us to obey, too. And just as rules at school and home keep us safe and happy, so do God's special rules. God gave us his rules to help us live and obey as he desires. Remember how God helped Moses lead the Israelites out of slavery in Egypt and across the Red Sea? Afterward, God led his**

people into the wilderness, where they wandered and wandered, afraid they were lost. The people forgot how much God loved them and began disobeying God. God decided his people needed special rules to keep them safe, healthy, happy, and obedient to him. So God called Moses up onto a mountain and gave Moses two stone tablets on which he had written ten special rules or commandments.

Let's learn those special rules right now. You can help identify the Ten Commandments. As I read each commandment, walk in a circle stepping on the rule cards each time you come to one. When I say, "Hey, hey—stop and obey," freeze in place. The person on or nearest the commandment I just read can clip the card to our clothesline.

Read each of the following commandments and after each one, stop and say, "Hey, hey—stop and obey." Have the child standing on or nearest the correct commandment read it aloud, then clip it to the clothesline.

Commandment 1: "I am your God. I am your only God."
Commandment 2: "You will not make any false images or idols."
Commandment 3: "You will not treat God's name badly."
Commandment 4: "Keep the Sabbath day holy."
Commandment 5: "Honor your mother and father."
Commandment 6: "Do not murder."
Commandment 7: "Do not steal."
Commandment 8: "Do not lie."
Commandment 9: "Do not desire someone else's husband or wife."
Commandment 10: "Don't wish for other people's things."

Count the commandments and point to each clip as you repeat the order once more. Then say: **What important rules to learn and follow! And it's wonderful to know that God gave us his special rules through his love and protection. Let's explore more about why God wants us to obey him and how the Ten Commandments can help us obey God.**

MAKING IT MEMORABLE

Have kids sit in front of the cards on the clothesline. Say: **God's commandments give us important rules for living, and if they are obeyed, we please God, live happily, and show our love for God. Let's see what the Bible says about obeying God's commandments and why it is so important to do so.** Invite volunteers to read aloud Deuteronomy 27:10 and 28:1. Then ask:

★ *Why do you think God gave us special rules to follow?*
★ *How do you think God feels when we disobey him? obey him?*
★ *How does obeying God keep us safe and happy?*

Read aloud 1 John 5:3, then ask:

★ *In what ways does obeying God's commands demonstrate our love for him?*

★ *How can we obey God more?*

Say: **Obeying God's commands isn't just the wise thing to do; it's the loving thing to do! When we choose to learn and obey God's Ten Commandments, we tell God we respect his rules and love him. Let's share a prayer thanking God for his rules to live and love by. When I come to the place to name God's rules, you can have a turn to read one of the commandments as a thank-you to God.**

Offer a brief prayer thanking God for giving us rules to live by and asking for his help in obeying them, then close by saying: **We thank you, Lord, for your commandment that says** (have kids each read commandments, repeating some if necessary). Close with a corporate "amen." If there's time, sing "God Is So Good."

Form ten groups and assign each group one of the Ten Commandments to illustrate using paper, markers, and crayons. Have kids write the words to their particular commandments on the illustrations. Then repeat the Ten Commandments aloud as groups clip their illustrations to the string clothesline. Choose one group of kids to scramble up the order of the pictures as the others hide their eyes. Then see if the rest of the class can unscramble the illustrations.

A FINE FEAST

Give thanks to God in all things!

Leviticus 23:40-43; Psalms 35:18; 69:30; 1 Thessalonians 5:18

BEFORE BEGINNING...

Before beginning, gather the Story Kit items. Since this is a Wow 'Em Bible story, you'll also need duct tape, wheat bread, honey butter or plain honey, oat cereal, dried dates (chopped), and raisins. In this pencil Bible-story presentation about the Feast of Tabernacles (or Tents), kids will be having a feast inside of their own tent made from the plastic shower curtain. To make the tent, use duct tape to tape two of the corners to the walls in one corner of the room. Tape the corners about 5 feet up the wall. Now, after spreading your tent as wide as it will go, tape the other two corners to sturdy chairs. Kids will be sitting inside the covered area to enjoy their feast and to learn about how God's people thanked him long ago and how we can thank him today. You'll be serving wheat bread on which kids can spread honey butter or plain honey using the plastic spoons. (Honey butter is recommended, since it doesn't drip as much.) You will also provide a lunch sack of raisins; one of dried, chopped dates; and one of oat cereal to symbolize the grains and fruits brought to the feast in Old Testament times. This story lesson is wonderful when told around Thanksgiving time.

Story Kit Supplies

❑ **Bible**
❑ **plastic shower curtain**
❑ **paper plates**
❑ **plastic spoons**
❑ **lunch sacks**

TELLING THE STORY

Be sure the tent is prepared and that you have raisins, dried dates, and oat cereal in the lunch sacks from the Story Kit. Set the paper plates in a stack inside the tent along with a plate of wheat bread and one on which you have the container of honey butter.

Gather kids outside of the tent and say: **Welcome! Today we have a special feast to celebrate and learn about. It's called the Feast of Tents or Tabernacles, and it was a favorite feast of God's people in Old Testament times. This feast was ordered by God as a way for his people to thank him for the**

29

blessings he gave them at harvest time. Remember, no one had a super-market or meat shop to visit when they needed food—they had to work hard to grow or harvest what they ate. And the people had to rely on God's grace and provision to give them the foods they needed to stay alive. Let's step into our tent to learn more about this special feast and to share good times, good friends, good food, and a lot of thanks to God!**

Have kids find places to sit under the tent. If you can position kids in an oval or circle, it works best. When everyone is seated, say: **God came to Moses and gave him instructions for the Feast of Tabernacles or Tents. God told the people to celebrate this thanksgiving feast for seven days, and during that time they were to live in booths or tents to remind them of how God had brought his people out of slavery in Egypt and had them live in booths or tents. God wanted the people to remember his blessings and to celebrate them with a feast of thanksgiving.**

Hand out the paper plates and plastic spoons. Continue: **The people loved this festival because they didn't have to work and could spend their time thanking God and sharing wonderful feasts! God told the people to bring fruits such as dates from the palm trees to eat. The people praised and thanked God for the juicy fruit he provided all year.**

Pass the sacks of raisins and dates. Have each child place one or two spoonfuls on his plate. Then continue: **The people also enjoyed good grains and breads and thanked God for these basic parts of the daily meals.** Pass the sack with the oat cereal and the wheat bread. Have kids take a slice of bread and a spoon-ful of oat cereal. Then say: **And they enjoyed sweet honey they collected and thanked God for the sweet goodness he gave them.** Pass around the honey butter and let kids each take a spoonful to put on their bread.

Say: **What a wonderful feast they all had in celebration of God's bless-ings. But of course they did something very special before they ate. What do you think they did? They thanked God with prayers! And so can we.** Invite several kids to pray and thank God for the blessings he brings our way every day. Then go around the tent and have each child name one thing he or she is espe-cially thankful for. End with a corporate "amen."

Invite kids to enjoy their meal as you chat about blessings God gives in different areas, such as in the foods we eat, the people in our lives, the schools and churches that help us learn, and other areas.

MAKING IT MEMORABLE

When kids are almost finished with their feast, read aloud Leviticus 23:40-43. Say: **God gave very specific directions for how he wanted the people long ago to thank him.** Ask:

★ *How do you think it makes God feel when we offer him our thanks?*

★ *What are ways we can thank God for his blessings?*

Say: **There are many ways to tell God thank you. One of those ways is through our prayers. Another way is through being kind to the people we meet each day. And another way is through reading God's Word. Let's see what the Bible says about giving thanks.** Invite volunteers to read aloud Psalms 35:18; 69:30; 100:4; 106:1; and 1 Thessalonians 5:18. Then ask:

★ *Why is it important to thank God in all things and not just for the food we eat?*

★ *How does having a heart filled with thanks show God our love for him?*

★ *What is one way you can thank God today for all he has done for you?*

Have kids go around the tent and tell one way they can thank God today for his love and rich blessings. Then say: **Another way to thank God is through song. Let's thank God for today and each day that we can enjoy his goodness, love, help, and blessings!**

Close by singing "This Is the Day the Lord Has Made" and any other songs you know that would praise and thank God in joyous ways.

Make a class cornucopia of God's blessings. Cut a large sheet of brown or yellow poster board into a circle and twist it into a cone shape. Tape the seam securely. Let kids make fruit-shape cutouts from construction paper, then on each piece of fruit, write a different thank-you to God by finishing this sentence: Dear God, I thank you for (blank) every day! Have kids fill the paper cone with the thank-you fruit shapes. Then each time you meet for the next several weeks, pull out several pieces of fruit and read the thanks-yous on them and offer a prayer to God thanking him for his blessings.

OUR MIGHTY GOD!

Our strength is found in God alone!

Exodus 15:2; Judges 16:4-30; Psalms 18:1, 2, 21:13, 28:7

BEFORE BEGINNING...

Story Kit Supplies

- ❏ Bible
- ❏ balloons
- ❏ permanent marker
- ❏ newspaper
- ❏ 1 plastic coin

Before beginning, gather the Story Kit items as well as the following classroom supplies: scissors and clear tape. Kids will love the unusual storytelling technique in this story lesson about Samson and the source of his strength. Make a balloon "Samson" by inflating a balloon and tying a knot in it. Use the permanent marker to draw Samson's face (remember, no beard!). Then cut many strips of newspaper and tape them to the top of the balloon for his hair. Make the strips quite long! Kids will be making their own Samson balloons to help tell the Bible story. They'll use scissors to give the Samsons haircuts (which they'll love!) and then learn where the real source of Samson's strength was—in God! (Note: You may wish to provide several more permanent markers and pairs of scissors to speed up your balloon facials and haircuts!)

TELLING THE STORY

Have the newspaper, scissors, tape, permanent marker, and a balloon for each child handy. Hold up the balloon head of Samson and say: **This is a pretend balloon-face of a man from the Old Testament. His name was Samson, and as you can see, he had very long hair! Samson never cut his hair because he had made a promise to honor God and always serve him, and Samson never cut his hair as a sign of his promise. Samson was a judge in Old Testament times and loved God very much. He was famous throughout the land for his awesome strength. Samson thought his strength was in his long hair, which was made into seven braids, though Samson never told anyone his secret! Let's make Samson heads like this one to help tell the rest of the exciting story of Samson and what happened when he leaked his secret to a sly woman who didn't love God.**

Have kids quickly make their Samson balloon faces and add the paper hair. After the balloons are finished, have kids sit in a circle. Keep several pairs of scissors handy. Retell the story of Samson and how his hair was cut from Judges 16:4-30: **God's enemies wanted to find out the secret source of Samson's strength, so they paid a woman named Delilah to get the secret out of Samson. Delilah nagged and nagged Samson to tell her his secret, and finally Samson gave in. Samson told Delilah that his strength was in his long hair. Then Delilah did an awful and wicked thing: She cut his long hair!**

Let kids cut the newspaper hair on their Samson balloons. As they snip away, say: **Samson told his secret, and his long hair, which had been the symbol of his promise to love and serve God, was gone—and so was his strength! God's enemies captured Samson and blinded the weak judge. They kept him in chains for a very long time—long enough for his hair to begin growing. And long enough for Samson to be sorry for what he had done. Samson prayed to God to help him take revenge on his enemies. So when Samson was chained between two pillars in the temple courtyard and many important people and soldiers were there—all of God's enemies—Samson prayed for God to make him strong once more. God heard his prayers, and Samson was so strong he pushed in the pillars and all God's enemies died. Samson died, too, but he had discovered at last that his strength was in God and in God alone!**

Have kids hold on to their Samson balloons, then say: **What an exciting story! Let's answer a few story questions, then read more about our source, of strength who is God and God alone.**

MAKING IT MEMORABLE

Have kids stand in a circle, then ask the following questions. If someone knows the answer, have him bop his Samson balloon up and down, then call on a volunteer to answer. Ask:

★ *Where did Samson think his strength was?*
★ *Who was really the source of his strength?*
★ *Why do you think God answered Samson's prayer and made him strong once more?*

Say: **Samson believed his strength was in his hair alone, but when he was held captive, Samson's hair grew back and he was still weak. Samson didn't regain his strength until he apologized to God and asked for his**

strength once more to serve God. That's when God decided to strengthen Samson once more. And Samson discovered the source of his strength was really in God! What a powerful lesson he learned, and we can learn that same lesson. Let's read what the Bible says about where our strength lies.

Form four groups and assign each group one of the following verses to read: Exodus 15:2; Psalm 18:1, 2; Psalm 21:13; and Psalm 28:7. Let kids choose one person in their group to be the reader and practice reading their portions of Scripture in rhythm as the other group members bop their Samson balloons in time to the chant. After several minutes of practice, let groups read their verses for the whole class. Then ask:

★ *Why is it wise to trust in God's power, might, and strength?*

★ *In what ways can we use our strength to serve God as Samson did?*

Say: **Samson learned a powerful lesson about the power of God and where his strength was. I'm glad that we know God alone is the source of our strength and help, aren't you?** Close by letting kids bop their balloons in time to the following rhyme.

God alone is my help and strength—
I never have to fear!
For the perfect power of God above
Is always standing near!

Let kids make God Is My Rock paperweights. Choose large, smooth stones and have kids paint "God is my strength … my rock!" on the stones using acrylic paints. When the paints are dry, spray the rocks with shellac, then glue squares of craft felt on the bottoms to prevent furniture scratches. Remind kids that we often think our help and strength lie in other people or things but that God is our only true source of strength!

RUTH'S BEST FRIEND

We want God to be a big part of our friendships.

Ruth 1:1-2:23; Ecclesiastes 4:9-12; 1 John 4:7-11

BEFORE BEGINNING...

*Before beginning, gather the Story Kit items as well
as markers. Since this is a Wow 'Em Bible Story, you'll
also need a festive gift bag and treats to place inside,
such as caramel corn, popcorn, small wrapped can-
dies, or small apples, one for each child. Before story
time, inflate three balloons and decorate them with
women's faces. Write "Naomi" on one balloon, "Ruth"
on another, and "Orpah" on the third. As you retell the
story of Ruth and Naomi, you'll be bopping balloons
around a circle. At the end of the story, everyone*
will sit in the circle and share their friendships and treats from the gift bag.

Story Kit Supplies

❑ **Bible**
❑ **balloons**
❑ **permanent markers**

TELLING THE STORY

Set the gift bag containing the treats off to one side. Have kids form two concen-
tric circles, then have kids in the inner circle walk in one direction as the kids in the
outer circle walk in the opposite direction. When you clap, have kids stop and greet
the person in the circle across from them with a handshake or high fives. After several turns, have kids form one large circle. Say: **Friends are such fun, aren't they?
Some friends are people we're friendly with and smile at but maybe don't
spend lots of time with. Other friends are true, deep-down friends with
whom we share our secrets, dreams, and hopes. True, best friends are gifts
from God and make the world a very nice place to live in! Today's Bible
story is about true friendship and how two women discovered who their
best friend was.**

Hold up the Naomi balloon and say: **It is the story of Naomi, a woman who
had two sons who married two young women.** (Hold up the Orpah and Ruth
balloons.) **One young woman was named Orpah, and the other, Ruth. As we
tell the story, we'll gently bop these character balloons around the circle,**

keeping track of which balloon is who. When I say "stop," hold on to the balloons and name the one you're holding. Then I'll ask a story question of one of the characters. If it is the balloon you're holding, you can answer the question.

Retell the story of Ruth and Naomi's friendship from Ruth 1, 2 as you bop around the balloons according to the directions in parentheses. Begin bopping the Naomi balloon as you say:

Naomi was an older woman who knew and loved God. She had two sons who married two young women named Orpah and Ruth. (Add in the Orpah and Ruth balloons and bop all three around the circle.) **Naomi loved both Orpah and Ruth, but Naomi and Ruth became especially good friends. Naomi taught Ruth all about God, and soon Ruth came to know and love God, too. Stop.** (Stop bopping the balloons.) Call on the person holding the Naomi balloon and ask:

★ **Why was it loving and good for Naomi to teach Ruth about God?**

Continue bopping the balloons and say: **Then something awful happened. Naomi's husband and sons died, and only Orpah, Ruth, and Naomi were left. Naomi kindly told Ruth and Orpah they could to return to their mothers if they wanted to go home. Ruth and Orpah cried. They loved Naomi and didn't want to leave her. Stop.** Call on the person holding the Ruth balloon and ask:

★ **Why did Ruth love her friend Naomi?**

Call on the person holding the Orpah balloon and ask:

★ **Why was it good for the three women to have friends when life became hard and lonely?**

Continue bopping the balloons and say: **Orpah finally decided to return to her mother and left.** (Remove the Orpah balloon so that only the Ruth and Naomi balloons are being bopped around the circle.) **Ruth told her friend Naomi, "Where you go, I will go, and your God will be my God." So Naomi and her friend Ruth went to the town of Bethlehem, where Naomi had other relatives. Stop.** Call on the person holding the Naomi balloon and ask:

★ **How did Naomi sharing God's love with Ruth bring the two friends closer together?**

Continue bopping the balloons and say: **When Ruth and Naomi arrived in Bethlehem, they were very hungry. Ruth wanted to help her friend Naomi, so she went to the fields to gather grain to bake into bread. Ruth picked grain and put it in her grain sack. Stop.** Call on the person holding the Ruth balloon and ask:

★ **Why did Ruth work for and want to help her friend Naomi?**

Place the gift bag in the center of the circle. Continue bopping the balloons and say: **When Ruth and Naomi sat down to share their friendship and their**

meal, they also shared a prayer thanking God for all his blessings. Stop. Set the balloons aside and share a prayer thanking God for good friends, then share the goodies in the sack. Say: **As we share our friendships and snacks, let's explore more about why God sends us special friends and how they help us draw closer to one another and to God.**

MAKING IT MEMORABLE

Invite volunteers to read aloud 1 John 4:7-11. Then ask:
★ *How does loving God allow us to love others?*
★ *Without love for God, can we really have friends to love? Explain.*
★ *How does sharing God with our friends draw us closer to them and to God?*

Invite several volunteers to read aloud Ecclesiastes 4:9-12. Then ask:
★ *Why are two friends better than one person alone?*
★ *Why does God send us special friends?*
★ *In what ways can best friends love and support one another?*
★ *Why is it important to make God the "third strand" in the cord of three with you and your best friend?*

Say: **Ruth discovered how loving and kind Naomi could be, especially when Naomi taught her about God and his love. Ruth went from not knowing God to being the mother of Obed, whom Jesus was descended from years later. That's amazing! What a good friend Naomi was! We can be just as good a friend to our friends, too, by keeping God as a big part of our friendships with others.** End by singing "What a Friend We Have in Jesus," then the old camp favorite, "Make New Friends" using the following words:

Make new friends but keep the old—
With God in the center, our friends are gold!

Kids will love making friendship shoelaces to share with their best friends. Let kids decorate pairs of white shoelaces using permanent markers and glitter glue. After the laces dry thoroughly, twirl them together to make a cord, then tie the ends with ribbons. Have kids give their gifts to their best friends as they remind them that God is in the center of their special cord of friendship.

GIANT BRAVERY!

God gives us the courage to stand for him.

Deuteronomy 31:6; Joshua 1:7, 9; 1 Samuel 17:4-8, 40-49

BEFORE BEGINNING...

Before beginning, gather the Story Kit items as well as the following classroom supplies: scissors, tape, and markers. Cut a 10-inch length of ribbon and one 3-foot-long and one 6-foot-long length of white shelf paper. Kids will be making story props during the retelling of the story of David and Goliath. The David group will make a 3-foot-tall paper David and sling. The Goliath group will make a 6-foot-tall Goliath with a shield. Since Goliath was a bit more than twice as tall as David, kids will have a good idea of their size difference! During the question and answer time, kids will throw masking-tape "stones" at the Goliath figure. This story lesson will lead kids in understanding that courage is not a matter of physical size but the size of faith and love for God.

Story Kit Supplies

❑ **Bible**
❑ **ribbon**
❑ **3 paper plates**
❑ **white shelf paper**
❑ **masking tape**
❑ **ribbon**

TELLING THE STORY

Place the Story Kit items, scissors, tape, and markers on the floor. Gather kids and ask:

★ *What does it mean to have courage?*
★ *When is a time you acted brave and courageous? Did anyone help you have courage? In what way?*

Say: **Being courageous isn't always easy! That's why it's important to trust God and to rely on his power and might to help us be brave. God gives us courage to help us stand up and fight for him and for his truth. Long ago, a boy named David learned that physical size doesn't matter to God—only the size of our faith and love for him! Let's work together to retell the exciting story of how David stood up for God against a mean giant.**

Have kids form two groups, the Davids and the Goliaths. Hand the Goliaths the larger piece of shelf paper and two paper plates. Hand the David group one paper plate, the piece of ribbon, and the shorter length of paper. Be sure each group has markers, scissors, and tape. Explain that as you retell the story, kids will be making the story props in their groups as you direct them.

Say: **Once there was a very nasty, very big soldier who didn't love God. He had a scraggly beard and was scowly and haughty because he thought he was bigger and better than God. Goliath might have been big, but his heart was very small. David, on the other hand, loved God very much. He was just a young shepherd lad with bright eyes. David wasn't very big— why, he didn't even have a beard yet! But David's love for God was giant-sized! Use your paper plates to quickly draw your character's face.**

Have kids work in their groups to quickly draw a scowly, bearded face for Goliath face and a young lad's face for David. Then have kids put down their markers and continue the story and your descriptions. Say: **Goliath spent each day laughing at God and calling him names. Oh, but it made David angry! Goliath dared anyone to fight for God, but all of God's soldiers were afraid of Goliath. After all, he was so big and had lots of armor and a big shield to protect him! But David's love and loyalty for God were giant-sized, and he took up Goliath's challenge! David didn't have any armor, but he did have his shepherd's sling—and he had God to protect him. Tape your character's head to the white paper, then draw your character's body.**

Guide kids in their drawings, reminding them that Goliath had a great deal of armor. Have kids make his shield from the second paper plate. Remind the David group that David only had his belted robe, but he did have a sling, which kids can fashion out of ribbon.

After a few minutes, tape the figures side by side on the wall. Say: **Wow! Goliath was so much bigger than David, but David's love for God was even bigger! David bravely took his sling and five smooth stones. David hurled one stone at the mean giant and wham—Goliath toppled to the ground, never to fight or live again! David won the battle because of the courage he had in God's power and might! Let's discover more about the bravery and courage God gives us to stand up and fight for him with our love and loyalty. We'll use this figure of Goliath to help.**

MAKING IT MEMORABLE

Have kids each make three "sticky stones" by wadding 8-inch pieces of masking tape into balls. Untape the figure of David and place him on the floor about 3 feet in front of the figure of Goliath on the wall. Have kids stand behind the figure of David and get ready to toss one of their sticky stones. Say: **We'll read a few verses, then I will ask three questions. If you know the answer to a question, toss one sticky stone at Goliath. The person who lands closest to his shield can answer that question.** Read aloud Deuteronomy 31:6 and Joshua 1:7, 9. Then ask:

★ *How does knowing that God will always be with us help us be brave and courageous?*

After the sticky stones have been tossed and the question answered, ask the next question and repeat the tossing and answering.

★ *Why do you think God wants us to be loyal and fight for him and with him against enemies?*

★ *Why is the size of our faith, love, and courage more important than how tall or big we are on the outside?*

After all the stones have been tossed, say: **David learned that courage comes from loving God and trusting in his help. We can take a lesson from David, too, and put our trust in God so we can always be brave and courageous in God's name. With God for us, who can ever be against us?** Share a prayer thanking God for giving you courage to stand for and with him against temptations, false teachings, and disobeying God. If there's time, sing "Awesome God."

Play a lively game of Topple the Giant. Form two groups and have kids stand at opposite ends of the room in two lines. Stand five paper lunch sacks from the Story Kit in the area between the groups. Toss the ball from the Story Kit back and forth as you try to topple the center sacks. Score one point for each side knocking over a sack. Continue play until one team has five points.

SHEPHERD'S SONG

The Lord is our shepherd and our peace.

Psalm 23; John 10:11, 14, 15

BEFORE BEGINNING...

Before beginning, gather the Story Kit items as well as the following classroom supplies: scissors, tempera or watercolor paints, brushes or cotton swabs, and two bowls of water. (If you choose not to use paints, substitute markers and crayons.) Cut a 5-foot-long piece of white shelf paper on which kids can paint (or color and draw) a mural to illustrate Psalm 23. Use tempera paints or watercolor paints—or if you want less mess, use crayons and markers and let kids draw and color in their designs. Kids will be working together to create a scene of the pastoral fields described in Psalm 23 as they discover that God is like a loving shepherd who cares for us, leads us, and brings us great joy and peace. (Note: If your class is large, you may wish to create several of murals to avoid "kid crowding" along the paper.)

Story Kit Supplies

- ❏ **Bible**
- ❏ **white shelf paper**
- ❏ **plastic shower curtain**
- ❏ **newspaper**

TELLING THE STORY

Spread the plastic shower curtain flat on the floor and place the white shelf paper on top. Spread newspapers on the floor and place the paints and water on the papers. Gather kids along one side of the mural and explain that you'll be reading a wonderful poem of love, thanks, and praise written by David to express his feelings to God. Tell kids that after you read the psalm once, you'll discuss what is being said in the psalm and then have a chance to create a beautiful mural of the psalm to give to someone who needs a reminder of God's peace in his or her life.

Read aloud Psalm 23, then invite kids to take turns reading verses from the beautiful psalm. When everyone has had a turn to read a verse, say: **What a beautiful poem of thanks and love David wrote to God. Before David was a king,** he had been a shepherd watching over his father's flocks of sheep. David knew all about the peace of the fields and valleys. David understood that a good shepherd watches over his flock and keeps them safe so that each sheep feels secure and trusts the shepherd. Ask:

★ *In what ways is God like our perfect shepherd?*

★ *How do we trust God as sheep trust their shepherd?*

Say: **Let's read a bit more from God's Word about how God brings us peace and in what ways he is like our perfect shepherd. Then you can start on your mural.**

MAKING IT MEMORABLE

Have volunteers read aloud Psalm 100:3 and John 10:11, 14, 15. Then ask:

★ *Why does a shepherd lay down his life for his sheep?*

★ *How is this like the way God gave his Son to save our lives?*

★ *In what ways does God bring us peace?*

★ *How can we thank God, like David, for being our shepherd who loves and cares for us?*

Say: **God brings our spirits peace and security. He knows us and was willing to give his Son's life to save us, just as a good shepherd would do. It's important to thank God each day for being our perfect shepherd and to celebrate being the sheep of his flock! We can thank God right now by making a mural to express our loving thanks. Work together to draw the peaceful pasture scene we read of in Psalm 23. Then when our mural is finished, we can give it to someone to enjoy as a reminder of God's peace.**

Let kids work to create their scene along the entire length of the mural. If you desire, some of the kids could write the words to Psalm 23 at one end of the

mural instead of making the scene travel the whole length of the paper. As kids work, you might consider playing soft, peaceful instrumental praise music as inspiration.

When the mural is completed, present it to someone in your church or community as a thank-you or as a lift and to remind that person of God's perfect peace in our lives. Close by prayerfully reading Psalm 23 once more in unison, then end with a corporate "amen."

Kids might enjoy making edible "sheep of his pasture." For each fluffy lamb, poke a large marshmallow with a toothpick, then dip the marshmallow in milk. Drop the marshmallow in a plastic sandwich bag filled with shredded coconut and shake the bag until the marshmallow sheep is coated with "fleece." Make several sheep to nibble on as you read John 10:11, 14, 15 again.

TREASURE HUNT!

God's Word is precious and to be obeyed.

2 Kings 22:1-11; Psalm 119:11, 16, 17; 2 Timothy 3:16, 17

BEFORE BEGINNING...

Before beginning, gather the Story Kit items as well as the following classroom supplies: scissors and markers. Cut a 10-inch length of ribbon or string and tie it around the Bible. Then hide the Bible in the room in a challenging place but in plain sight. You'll be spreading the plastic shower curtain on the floor and scattering the items from the Story Kit around the curtain and floor for kids to clean up at the appropriate time. Kids will also go on a treasure hunt for God's Word and seek the Bible with the ribbon or string tied around it. This story lesson will help kids realize that God's Word is to be respected, honored, learned, and obeyed. (Note: If you have access to different Bible versions, especially older Bibles, bring them in for children to carefully look through. Compare and contrast how Bibles are alike and different.)

Story Kit Supplies

❏ **Bible**
❏ **paper plates**
❏ **1 empty pop can**
❏ **1 jingle bell**
❏ **six clothespins**
❏ **plastic shower curtain**
❏ **index cards**
❏ **ribbon or string**

TELLING THE STORY

Spread the shower curtain on the floor, then scatter the items from the Story Kit over the curtain and around it on the floor. Be sure you've previously hidden the Bible with the ribbon or string tied around it. Then gather kids and ask:

★ ***What's your favorite book? Why?***

Say: **Did you know that one of the best gifts we've been given is a book? That's right! God gave us this precious gift of the Bible—his Word. But the Bible wasn't always in a book form as we know it. Long ago, God's Word was written on paper scrolls and kept in his temple. You'd think such a precious gift as God's Word wouldn't become lost or misplaced, but that's what happened long ago. Let's hear an exciting story about a young king**

and the wonderful treasure-book he found. **You can help tell the story by following my directions, so listen carefully!**

King Josiah was only a boy, but he loved God in a big way! Josiah honored God and wanted to learn all he could about our heavenly Father and how to obey him the best he could. Though Josiah loved and honored God, he was sad because God's chosen people had not been obeying God or honoring him. In fact, the temple of the Lord had been strewn with junk and needed lots of repairs. When Josiah was older, he ordered God's temple cleaned and repaired. Let's pretend this is God's temple and help clean it up. Toss the items you find to one another, then into this Story Kit box.

Allow a few minutes to let kids toss the items to each other, then into the box. When everything is cleaned, give each other high fives before continuing: **As the temple was being cleaned, Josiah's men found a wonderful treasure tied with a string. See if you can hunt around the room to find something tied with a string** (or ribbon). **When you find it, bring it back to our shower-curtain temple.**

When the Bible is placed in the center of the shower curtain, have everyone sit around the edges. Then say: **King Josiah's men found the most important and powerful gift God has given us besides Jesus! When King Josiah unwrapped the scroll, he discovered it was God's Word! The people hadn't been reading or obeying God's Word all this time because the scroll had been lost. King Josiah wanted the people to know what God's Word said, so he read the scroll to everyone. Then King Josiah and all the people promised something about God's Word: They promised to learn it and say it and always obey it! And we can, too! Let's explore more about God's Word and why it is the best book gift we could ever have been given and why we should learn it and say it and always obey it!**

MAKING IT MEMORABLE

Untie the string or ribbon from the Bible. Have kids form three groups and assign each group one of the following verses to read from Psalms: 19:14; 119:16; and 119:17. Have kids decide whether their verses say to learn it or say it or always obey it when it comes to God's Word. Then have groups read aloud their verses and tell what they think the verse is teaching them about God's Word. Say: **God's Word teaches us that to please God, we want to learn his Word, repeat**

and use his Word, and always obey his Word. In this way, we live as God desires. What can God's Word do for us when we learn it and say it and always obey it? Let's find out!

Read aloud Psalm 119:9, 11, 74, and 2 Timothy 3:16, 17. Then ask:

★ *How do learning and knowing God's Word help us obey him?*
★ *Why is God's Word a good blueprint to follow for our lives?*
★ *In what ways can reading the Bible help us every day?*
★ *How can you thank God for his Word this week?*

Say: **Josiah knew that God's Word is to be respected, honored, and obeyed, and we know that it's pleasing to God when we learn it and say it and always obey it!** Close by singing "The B-I-B-L-E." Write the letters to spell the word *Bible* on index cards from the Story Kit and let younger kids flash the cards as they sing to help them remember how to spell this important word.

Turn God's Word into a colorful craft project. Dip the edges of folded paper towels into food coloring to give them a tie-dyed appearance. Open the paper towels and set them aside to dry flat. Invite kids to read over Psalm 119 for a verse they especially like. Write the verses on small squares of colored construction paper, then tape the verses to the centers of the dried paper towels.

FAITHFUL DANIEL

God is faithful to us when are faithful to him.

Psalms 25:10; 100:5; 117:2; Proverbs 28:20; Daniel 6:7-27

BEFORE BEGINNING...

Before beginning, gather the Story Kit items as well as the following classroom supplies: scissors, and markers or crayons. In this lively Bible story, kids will be making impromptu costumes for Daniel, the lions, and King Darius using paper plates, newspapers, and markers or crayons. Before class, cut the center circles from paper plates, preparing one plate for each child and one for yourself. Finish preparing the one for yourself to show as a sample. On one side of the plate, draw a headband and hair such as Daniel might have had. On the other side, tape a fringe of newspaper strips around the plate as a lion's mane. To represent the king, kids will simply place the plates on their heads as crowns. This fun and fanciful story technique will help kids learn that Daniel was faithful to God and continued to pray no matter what the cost! They'll also discover that God was also faithful to Daniel's obedience.

Story Kit Supplies

❏ **Bible**
❏ **paper plates**
❏ **newspapers**
❏ **masking tape**

TELLING THE STORY

Gather children on the floor and hold the paper-plate mask to your face, Daniel side showing. Say: **I have a riddle for you. See if you can guess what Bible story I am describing.** Read the following riddle and quickly change plate positions as you read.

> *I told God I'd always pray,* (Daniel side out)
> *Even if wild animals barred the way!* (lion side out)
> *No matter what the kings might say,* (plate on head as crown)
> *I'd be faithful to God all the way!* (Daniel side out)

When kids tell that it's the story of Daniel, say: **What an exciting story! Let's make masks and you can help retell the excitement of kings and lions and how God saved the day in a miraculous way!** Distribute the paper plates with the centers removed. Let kids quickly prepare their masks using your mask as a guide.

When the masks are complete, say: **It looks as if you're ready to tell the exciting story, so let's go. Each time I say the name "Daniel," quickly hold up your Daniel mask, drop to your knees, and pretend to pray. Each time I say the word "king," quickly hold your mask on your head as a crown. And each time I say "lions," hold up your lion mask and growl.** Begin the story and pause after each italicized word.

Once there was a man named *Daniel* who loved God and prayed only to him. But *King* Darius made a law that people were to pray only to him! The *king* ordered anyone praying to God to be put in a den with hungry *lions*. What should *Daniel* do? Should he pray to the *king* or to God? *Daniel* loved God, but he was afraid of the mean *lions*. What would you do? Allow time for kids to share their responses, then continue.

Daniel made his choice. He decided to keep praying to God, *lions* or no *lions! Daniel* loved God and wanted to obey him, *king* or no *king!* So when *King* Darius discovered *Daniel* praying to God, he shouted, "Into the *lions'* den!" All night long *Daniel* prayed for God to keep him safe—and God heard *Daniel's* prayers. God sent an angel to close the *lions'* jaws, and when the *king* came back in the morning, he was surprised to see *Daniel* alive and knew that *Daniel's* God was more powerful than anyone or anything. *King* Darius made a new law that day that said all the people should pray to *Daniel's* God, for God is mighty and powerful!

Have kids set aside their masks, then say: **Daniel was faithful to God, and in return God was faithful to Daniel. There is great power in prayer and great love in being faithful to God. Let's explore more about being faithful to God and how his faithfulness remains with us.**

MAKING IT MEMORABLE

Invite volunteers to read aloud Psalm 25:10; 100:5; 117:2; and 145:13. Then ask:
★ *Why do you think God was faithful and saved Daniel?*
★ *Do you think Daniel made a good choice to be faithful to God? Explain.*
★ *How long does God's faithfulness last? Explain.*
★ *Why does God desire us to be faithful and obedient?*

Say: **God is faithful to us when he knows our hearts and faith are in the right place. Daniel demonstrated his love, obedience, and faithfulness to God when he refused to stop praying or to pray to a false idol. Daniel remained faithful to God even though his life was threatened. And God remained faithful to Daniel! Listen to what God's Word teaches us about being faithful to God.** Read aloud Proverbs 28:20, then ask:

★ *Why do you think God blesses those who are faithful to him?*
★ *In what ways can you be faithful to God this week?*

Say: **God knows that when we are faithful to him by learning his Word, reading the Bible, honoring Jesus, praying, and being kind to others, we are telling God, "I love you." And because God loves us so greatly, he is faithful to us in giving us help, guiding our lives, teaching us, and forgiving us when we do wrong. Let's honor God's faithfulness with a song telling how good, great, and faithful God remains!** Sing "God Is So Good," then add another verse with the words, "God is so faithful."

Play a lively game of Daniel dodge ball. Clear a playing area in the room and stick a masking-tape line down the center of the floor. Have kids form two teams and stand on either side of the center line. Tell kids the Story Kit ball is a pretend lion. Let kids toss the ball back and forth (below waist level). If the "lion" touches anyone on the fly or if a player who catches the lion drops it, that person joins the other side. Play for five minutes or until only one person is left on a side.

GOD SAVES JONAH

Our prayers rise sweetly to God's ears and heart.

Psalm 66:19; Isaiah 41:10; Jeremiah 33:3; Jonah 1-3

BEFORE BEGINNING...

Before beginning, gather the Story Kit items. Since this is a Wow 'Em Bible Story, you'll also need the following items: cotton balls, three plastic vials with snap-on lids (available free at most pharmacies), and the following scented oils or liquids: tuna-fish oil, vinegar or pickle juice, and perfume or potpourri oil. Soak a cotton ball in each liquid or oil and place it in a vial. (Keep track of which vial contains the perfume or potpourri oil.) Snap the lids on tightly. Kids will be using their sense of smell to see what kinds of things might have been inside the fish that swallowed Jonah. Before story time, drape the shower curtain over a table or several chairs to make a hollow area where you can sit with the kids. Tape the curtain in place. This will be the make-believe belly of the fish. Through this fun and lively Bible-story lesson, kids will discover that, just as Jonah's prayers rose sweetly to God, each of our prayers reaches God's ears and heart.

Story Kit Supplies

❑ **Bible**
❑ **plastic shower curtain**
❑ **masking tape**

TELLING THE STORY

Be sure the shower-curtain "fish" is set up in one area of the room. Gather kids across the room and ask kids to tell about times they might have asked someone for help and received it. Encourage kids to tell how they felt when help arrived. Then say: **God shows his love in many ways, but one of the best is through his grace. "Grace" means we don't deserve God's goodness but he gives it to us anyway. And it's through God's loving grace that he hears and answers each of our prayers. In our Bible story today, a man named Jonah learned about God's grace and the power of prayer in an amazing way. It all began when God told Jonah to go to the town of Nineveh and tell the people there to obey God. But Jonah said, "Oh, no! I won't go!" And he hid**

from God! Do you think God knew where Jonah was hiding? Pause for kids to share their thoughts, then say: **You can help tell the rest of the story, but you'll need lots of energy and imagination! Ready? Follow me!**

Read the following rhyme based on the story of Jonah and the big fish. Encourage kids to follow your actions.

> ***Jonah was naughty and hid from God*** (waggle your finger)
> ***On a little fishing boat.*** (lock fingers to make a "boat")
> ***But when a storm made the boat rock and roll,*** (sway back and forth)
> ***Jonah jumped in the sea for a float.*** (jump in the pretend sea)
> ***Jonah didn't float like the ol' fishing boat—*** (sink slowly to the floor)
> ***Down he sank … glip, glip, glup!*** (plug your nose)
> ***Jonah sank down 'til he thought he would drown—*** (sink to your knees)
> ***Then a huge fish swallowed him up!*** (crawl into the shower-curtain fish)

Pause for a moment, then quietly say: **Ooo, Jonah was saved from drowning when God sent a big fish to swallow him. God showed his grace by saving Jonah even when Jonah had disobeyed God. But just think what it must have smelled like in that fish's belly! Cup your hands over your eyes and peer around. It was dank and dark, and it must have smelled pretty awful! What do you think it was like?** Have kids close their eyes, then pass around the vials of tuna oil and vinegar for them to smell. Say: **Pffew! There were lots of funny smells! But there was something that was sweet inside that big fish. It had a very pleasing scent. What could it be?** Pass around the vial containing the perfume or potpourri oil. Then say: **It was the sweet scent of prayers rising to God! Jonah knew he had been disobedient, so he prayed to God. For three days and nights, Jonah prayed and told God how sorry he was and asked for God's help. And those prayers rose like a sweet scent to God—and God answered Jonah's prayers!** Set aside the vials and continue the story rhyme.

> ***Jonah prayed in that fish for three days and nights.*** (hold up 3 fingers)
> ***He told God he was sorry and expressed his deep love,*** (make prayer hands)
> ***And every prayer rose like sweetest perfume*** (slowly lift your hands)
> ***To our heavenly Father above!*** (point upward)
> ***God heard and answered Jonah's prayers*** (nod your head)
> ***And made the fish spit Jonah on the sand—*** (crawl out of the fish)
> ***Then Jonah ran straight to Nineveh*** (jog in place)
> ***To tell people, "Keep God's commands!"*** (point upward)

Have kids sit in place, then say: **Jonah was very naughty when he disobeyed God, but he certainly learned his lesson! God showed Jonah his grace when he sent the fish to swallow Jonah and save him from drowning. And God showed his grace to Jonah when he heard and answered Jonah's prayers and set him free to go to Nineveh. Jonah learned that God hears and answers each of our prayers. Let's discover more about the power of prayer and how God hears and answers in his time and way.**

MAKING IT MEMORABLE

Invite volunteers to read aloud Psalm 66:19, Isaiah 41:10, and Jeremiah 33:3. Then ask:

★ *Why does God take time to listen to our prayers?*

★ *In what way does God show his love for us by hearing and answering our prayers?*

★ *How does praying express our love to God?*

★ *How does it strengthen you to know that God promises to help us when we come to him in prayer?*

Say: **Just as God heard and answered Jonah's prayers, God hears and answers our prayers. But God chooses the time he will answer and the way he will answer. Jonah might have thought God would just make him awaken in his comfy bed, but God chose to answer by having the fish spit him on the sand. God knows best how and when to answer our prayers, but we can be assured that he does hear and will answer each of our prayers. Let's offer God a prayer of thanksgiving right now for being so loving and attentive to our prayers.**

Share a prayer thanking God for hearing and answering prayer, then sing the following song to the tune of "B-I-N-G-O":

Every night and every day,
We can bow our hearts and pray!
God will hear our prayers—
God will hear our prayers—
God will hear our prayers—
And answer each one, too!

Have a fun treat as kids retell the story of Jonah. Provide cups of sweet "seawater" (apple juice) and fish-shaped crackers. Encourage kids to go around the table and each supply a part of the Bible story as they use their treats to help. When you're finished nibbling, have kids pretend the trash can is a giant fish and toss their empty cups in its tummy!

PERFECT PROMISE

God's promises are woven throughout our lives.

Joshua 23:14; Isaiah 9:7; Luke 2:1-7; 2 Corinthians 1:20

BEFORE BEGINNING...

Story Kit Supplies

❏ Bible
❏ ball of string

Before beginning, gather the Story Kit items as well as the following classroom supplies: scissors, newsprint, markers, and tape. In this simple but effective storytelling lesson, kids will toss a ball of string around a circle and weave the string, and themselves, together. Cut a 10-inch length of string, but keep the ball of string intact for the Bible story. The woven string will help kids realize that God weaves his promises, his Word, and his love into our lives. After the story poem about the promise of Jesus and his birth, kids will use the Bible to look up some of God's promises and write them in a list. Then they will look at which promises God has already kept and which he will keep in the future.

TELLING THE STORY

Be sure the newsprint is taped to a wall or door so kids can see it. Have a marker near the paper. Set the ball of string beside you and hold the piece of string. Gather kids in a circle, then say: **Let's pretend this string represents a promise someone made to you. This promise is strong and whole right now, isn't it?** (Tug on the piece of string to show it isn't broken or weak.) **But what happens if a promise is broken?** Have a volunteer break the string (or cut it with scissors). Then say: **A broken promise isn't strong and whole. And if you try to mend it** (tie a simple knot in the string, then have two kids pull the ends so the string comes apart again), **it just doesn't work as well. Promises need to be kept unbroken to be good, true, and trustworthy. Let's use this ball of string to discover what one of God's greatest promises was and if he kept that promise to us. After each line of the story poem, I'll hold on to this string and toss it to someone who can repeat the line. Then that person** will toss the string to someone else after I read the next line, and so on. Each time you toss the string, hold on to it as you toss it, and you'll soon see a woven pattern appear!

Read the following story rhyme based on Isaiah 9:7; Micah 5:2; and Luke 2:1-7 as you toss the ball of string after each line.

> *God made a promise to everyone:*
> *He would send the world his only Son.*
> *God knew the world needed forgiveness and love,*
> *So he promised a Savior from heaven above.*
> *For oh so long the people waited on God's Word—*
> *Would God ever keep the promise they had heard?*
> *And then one still and starry night,*
> *Shepherds saw a brilliant light.*
> *They heard the sweetest voices sing*
> *And saw the most amazing thing!*
> *God sent his angels just before morn*
> *To tell the shepherds, "Christ is born!*
> *Go and find the tiny Savior in Bethlehem*
> *For he's come to save and love all men!"*
> *Then the shepherds rejoiced in what they had heard*
> *And knew God keeps his promises and his Word!*

Stop tossing the ball of string and have kids look at the pattern. Say: **Wow! Our pattern looks almost like a star. It reminds me of the star in the sky the night Jesus was born. God promised us a Savior and kept his promise when he sent Jesus to love and forgive us. God always keeps his promises, and he makes sure that his promises to us become part of our lives with him! God weaves his love and truth into the promises he makes us, just as he did when he promised and sent Jesus. Let's explore more of God's promises and find out if he has kept them.** Have kids drop the string in the places they were standing so the pattern stays intact.

MAKING IT MEMORABLE

Gather kids by the newsprint on the wall. Explain that you will form four groups and read verses that tell about promises God has made. Read the verses, then decide if that promise has been kept yet or if we are still waiting. When each group has finished, have them read their verses aloud and share their thoughts on if the promise has been kept. List the promises and whether they have been kept yet or not on the newsprint. Assign each group one of the following verses to read: Genesis 9:14, 15 (the rainbow and promise never to destroy all life through a flood again); Genesis 17:19 (the promise of Isaac); Exodus 6:1

54

(promise to set the Israelite slaves in Egypt free); and John 14:2, 3 (Jesus' promise of a new place in heaven for us).

After sharing the verses and promises, ask:

★ *Why do you think God keeps his promises?*

★ *In what way did keeping his promise of a Savior give hope to the world? demonstrate God's love for us?*

★ *How do God's promises strengthen our faith in him? strengthen our hope for the future?*

Stand and look at your pattern once more, then read aloud 2 Corinthians 1:20 and Joshua 23:14. Then say: **God weaves his love and promises into our lives. When God kept his word to Noah and Abraham and the Israelites, his promises were woven into our lives in faith and trust. When God promised us the birth of Jesus, forgiveness and love have been woven throughout our lives. And when Jesus promises us a place in our "someday" heavenly home, hope has been woven into our lives. Let's hold the string pattern as we share a prayer thanking God for his promises that are always kept and become a part of our hearts and lives.**

Share a prayer, then close by singing "The First Noel" and "I Am a Promise." Then cut the story string into pieces to tie on each other's fingers as reminders that God always keeps his promises.

Make pretty Promise Pockets to remind children that God always keeps his promises. Set out colored envelopes, glitter glue, shiny star stickers, and markers. Invite children to write "God's Promise Pocket" on their envelopes, then use the craft materials to decorate the envelopes. Encourage kids to keep the envelopes in their Bibles. As they learn more about God's and Jesus' promises, write the promises on slips of paper to keep in the envelopes and to read often. You may wish to begin by listing the promises kids looked up and read about in the story lesson.

JESUS IS BORN

Jesus was God's gift and sacrifice of love!

Luke 2:1-7; John 3:16, 17

BEFORE BEGINNING...

Before beginning, gather the Story Kit items as well as a stapler, scissors, and markers. Since this is a Wow 'Em Bible Story, you will also need a festive gift bag, self-adhesive bows (one per child), and a small gift for each child that will be a reminder of Jesus, such as a pocket Bible, a cross to wear, or a WWJD bracelet. Place each gift in a lunch sack and staple it closed, then add festive self-stick bows to the packages. Cut the ribbon from the Story Kit into nine 10-inch lengths. Use sticky tack to attach the Picture Props to the ends of the ribbons, one picture per ribbon. Use a permanent marker to number the ribbon ends as follows: #1 and #2 (the man and woman); #3 (the angel); #4 (the donkey); #5, #6, #7 (the cow, dove, and sheep); #8 (the star); and #9 (the baby). Place the Picture Props in the festive gift bag with the ribbon ends hanging out so you can see the numbers as you tell the story. Use a bit of sticky tack to attach the ribbon ends to the sides of the bag so they don't slip inside. Kids will be passing the gift bag around the circle as the story is told and will be pulling surprise ribbons from the bag at appropriate times. In this story lesson, kids will realize that Christmas isn't the only time we celebrate and welcome Jesus—we welcome him each day with a celebratory heart and spirit!

Story Kit Supplies

- ❏ Bible
- ❏ lunch sacks (1 per child)
- ❏ ribbon
- ❏ sticky tack
- ❏ Picture Props (man, woman, baby, angel, star, donkey, cow, dove, sheep)

TELLING THE STORY

Have kids sit in a circle. Set the gift bag with the ribbons and pictures beside you. Then place the kids' gift bags in the center of the circle with the markers. Invite kids to briefly tell about the most special gifts they've ever given and how the people receiving those gifts felt. Say: **It's always lots of fun to *receive* gifts** but even more fun when we have something special to *give* to someone we love. **Did you know God gave up what he loved most at the same time he gave us the most special gift we'll ever receive? Let's discover what his gift was. We'll use this colorful gift bag to help, then see what gifts are for you in the bags in the center of the circle!**

Explain to kids that you'll pass around the gift bag and when you say "stop," whoever is holding the bag can pull out and reveal the first numbered ribbon and so on. As each ribbon is revealed, stick the Picture Prop on the wall so kids can see the order of them during the story. Retell the story of the first Christmas below from Luke 2:1-7 and Matthew 2:1, 2.

Joseph was a poor carpenter from the town of Nazareth. Stop. (Have the child holding the gift bag pull out and reveal ribbon #1, then stick the picture to the wall.) **Joseph loved God, and he also loved a young woman named Mary. Stop.** (Reveal picture #2 and stick it to the wall beside the first picture.) **Mary and Joseph were traveling to Bethlehem with a wonderful secret, but they knew that time was short and that they had to hurry. An angel of the Lord had told Mary she would soon have a special baby who would save the world from sin and death. Stop.** (Reveal picture #3.) **The angel told Mary that God would send a precious gift to the world and Mary would be his mother. Mary rode on the back of a donkey while Joseph walked beside them. Stop.** (Reveal picture #4.)

When Mary and Joseph came to Bethlehem, they looked for a place to stay—but there was no room at the inn. In fact, there was no room any-where! But God was with them, and Joseph spotted a stable where the animals slept. What animals were in the stable? One was munching on hay with a "moo." Stop. (Reveal picture #5.) **Another had feathers and always sang, "coo." Stop.** (Reveal picture #6.) **There were other animals, too, including donkeys and sheep. Stop.** (Reveal picture #7.)

God placed a bright star over the stable as a sign that something won-derful was about to happen. (Reveal picture #8.) **Then, in the still of the night, God's gift of love was sent to the world.** (Reveal picture #9.) **Baby Jesus was born in the still of the night, and Mary wrapped him in cloths and laid him in a manger. God gave up what he most loved because he loved us so great-ly. God gave us his Son Jesus as our Savior, friend, teacher, and Lord! What a perfect gift of love! Let's discover more about why God chose Jesus as his gift of love. Then we'll open the gifts in the center of the circle.**

MAKING IT MEMORABLE

Invite two volunteers to read aloud John 3:16 and 17. Then ask:
★ *Why did God give his only Son to a sinful world?*
★ *Why is Jesus God's most precious gift of love to us?*
Say: **God loved Jesus so very much, but God knew the world needed a Savior and the immense love that only Jesus could give. And even though God knew Jesus would have to die for us someday, he willingly gave us the precious gift of his own Son. Imagine—God loved us so greatly that he gave his only Son to love us and save us from sin and eternal death. There could never be such a gift of love in all the world!** Ask:
★ *How do you think God felt when Jesus was born? Explain.*
★ *How does it feel to know that God gave you his most precious gift of love?*
★ *In what ways can you thank God for the gift of Jesus?*
Lead kids in repeating John 3:16 several times, then offer a prayer thanking God for the gift of Jesus and the sacrifice of love he made when he unselfishly gave Jesus to the world. Then say: **God gave us the gift of his only Son even when he knew Jesus would give his life for us one day. Let's open the gifts in the center to remind us of how God freely gave us his gift of Jesus.** Open the gift bags, then close by singing, "The Friendly Beasts" using the Picture Prop pictures of the cow, donkey, sheep, and dove.

Play a game using self-adhesive bows from the kids' gift bags. Form two lines facing each other and about 5 feet apart. Start tossing or passing bows from one end of one line and the opposite end of the other line in a zigzag fashion between the lines. As you zigzag, have kids say, "Jesus is our gift of love," calling out one word each time a bow is tossed or passed. See if you can make the bows travel from one end of the line to the other, then back again.

WHERE IS JESUS?

Even teachers need to learn about Jesus.

Deuteronomy 31:12; Psalm 25:4, 5; Luke 2:42-51

BEFORE BEGINNING...

Before beginning, gather the Story Kit items as well as the following classroom supplies: scissors, markers, and clear tape. Cut a 2-foot length of white shelf paper and on it write the Greek word for "God" (see margin below). Tape the paper to the wall where kids can see it. Hide the picture of Jesus either in the pastor's study (ask permission first, of course) or tape the picture to his closed door. In this Bible story about young Jesus at the temple, kids will be "searching" for Jesus throughout your church. This Bible story lesson will help kids realize that we're never too old or wise to stop learning about God, that even teachers, pastors, and parents must always keep learning about the Lord. Kids will also learn how to write the Greek word for "God."

Story Kit Supplies

❏ Bible
❏ index cards
❏ white shelf paper
❏ Picture Prop (Jesus)

ΘЄΟS

TELLING THE STORY

Be sure the picture of Jesus is hidden in the pastor's office or taped outside on the closed door. Gather kids in the classroom and ask if they've ever lost or misplaced something very precious or dear to them, such as a pet, toy, blanket, or teddy bear. Encourage kids to tell how it felt to know their treasure was lost and how it felt to find that valued item. Then say: **When Jesus was very young, his parents lost him in a crowd of people. They were frantic! But they were also surprised when they found where he was and what he was doing. It was time for the Passover Feast in Jerusalem, and thousands of people from all over went to town for the celebration and feast. Jesus' parents, Mary and Joseph, took Jesus along to the feast, but walking on their way home, they noticed he was missing. They thought Jesus was with friends or relatives, but when they realized he was lost, they became very worried! They made their way back**

59

into the crowded city to look for Jesus. Let's go on our own hunt for Jesus. When you see Jesus, or at least a picture of him, shout, "Jesus is here!"

Take kids on a roundabout tour of the church, in and out of rooms, and even outside if the weather is nice. End up at the pastor's office and wait for someone to spy the hidden picture. Then either gather there or take the picture of Jesus back to the classroom. Say: **Jesus' parents were so glad to have found their precious boy! But they wondered what Jesus had been doing. Well, Jesus, who was only a boy, had been sitting with the elders of the temple and teaching them about God! Imagine—a young boy teaching the teachers about God! Jesus had taught them with understanding and wisdom, and everyone was amazed. Mary asked Jesus why he had come to the temple. And Jesus said to Mary and Joseph, "Why were you searching for me? Didn't you know I had to be in my Father's house?" But they didn't understand all that Jesus meant. What do you think Jesus meant?**

Allow time for kids to share their responses, then say: **Jesus knew the most natural place for him to be was near his heavenly Father, in his temple or house. And Jesus also knew the teachers had much to learn about God. God sent Jesus to teach us, and that is just what Jesus was doing! Let's see if we can discover why it's so important to learn about God and what things we must learn.**

MAKING IT MEMORABLE

Gather kids by the shelf paper with the Greek word for "God" written on it. Say: **This is something Jesus learned and may have even taught others. It is the Greek word for "God," and it is pronounced THEH-os. In a few minutes, we'll learn how to write this word, too. But first, let's see what Jesus might have been teaching the teachers in the temple—things we all need to learn about God.** Read aloud and Deuteronomy 31:12, and explain that an "alien" in the verse means a person from a different country. Then ask:

★ *What two things does this verse tell us to learn?*
★ *Why is it important to learn awe and respect, or reverence, for God?*
★ *Why is it important to learn to obey God's laws?*

Say: **Jesus knew how very important it is for us to respect God and revere him. This means that we're to fear God, not in a scary way, but in knowing he is all-powerful and is to be obeyed and respected above all else. What else might Jesus have been teaching the teachers? Let's see.** Read aloud Psalm 25:4, 5. Ask

★ *Why do we need to learn God's ways and how he wants us to act?*
★ *In what ways is it important to learn God's truth through reading, understanding, and using his Word?*

Say: **Jesus also knew the importance of knowing God's truths and what he says to us. In these ways, we can better understand what God desires and how to obey him. We all know kids go to school to learn. But teachers must also learn so they can be good teachers. Jesus could have just stopped outside of the temple to chat with passersby, but instead he chose to go into the temple and listen to the teachers and teach them.** Ask:

★ *In what ways did teaching the teachers show that Jesus cared for them?*

★ *Why do you think Jesus wants us to keep learning about God?*

Distribute the index cards and markers and teach kids how to write the Greek word for "God." Then have kids tape the cards to their shirts as name tags and tell everyone who asks that they learned how to write God's name in Greek and that we should all continue learning about God, as Jesus did, for a lifetime! End by singing "God Is So Good" if there's time.

Let kids draw and cut out block letters to the Greek word for "God" from colorful construction paper. Glue the letters to 3-foot lengths of white shelf paper, then embellish the letters with sequins, glitter glue, or other crafty tidbits. Challenge kids to hang these name posters in their rooms and to write on the posters each new thing they learn or each Scripture verse they read about God for the next several weeks.

WHATTA MIRACLE!

Jesus can do anything because all power is his!

Matthew 28:18; John 2:1-11; Philippians 3:20, 21

BEFORE BEGINNING...

Before beginning, gather the Story Kit items. Since this is a Wow 'Em Bible story, you'll also need a self-sealing plastic sandwich bag and drinking straw for each person, a pitcher or two of water, a large package of presweetened grape soft-drink mix, and a plate of small crackers or cookies to share. You'll also need several more permanent markers, since kids will be writing a rhyme on the balloons. (Make sure the sandwich bags are the self-locking type!) Kids will be hearing the story of Jesus' first miracle at Cana, where he miraculously changed water into wine. You'll set a party theme for this story in honor of the wedding celebration Jesus and his mother attended. Spread the shower curtain "tablecloth" on the floor and scatter balloons around
the room. (Make sure there is a balloon for each child.) Place the plate of crackers or cookies in the center of the shower curtain. During the storytelling, kids will be changing their own plain water to a delicious grape soft drink as they learn about Jesus being given ultimate power and authority to perform miraculous wonders.

Story Kit Supplies

- ❏ Bible
- ❏ plastic shower curtain
- ❏ 1 plastic spoon
- ❏ balloons
- ❏ permanent marker

TELLING THE STORY

Be sure the shower curtain is spread out on the floor and that the balloons are scattered around in a festive way. Set the plate of refreshments in the center of the shower-curtain tablecloth. Gather kids near the party area and say: **Wow! It looks like some sort of celebration. I wonder what we're celebrating today? Well, let's use this party motif to help retell the story of a time Jesus and his mother went to a wedding celebration in the town of Cana. You'll need these items for the party preparations.** Distribute the empty sandwich bags and drinking straws. **We'll act out the story as we go.**

Jesus and his mother Mary had been invited by their friends to a wedding celebration in Cana. The party was so nice with lots of people and friendly chatter. (Have kids greet one another and shake hands.) **There was good grape wine to sip** (have kids pretend to sip through their drinking straws) **and tasty foods to sample.** (Pretend to munch on cookies and cakes.) **Yes, you could always tell a good host and hostess by the amount of refreshments they had, and Jesus' friends were proud of their nice party—that is, until the wine ran out.** (Hold the straws upside down and shake them.)

Jesus' friends were so embarrassed, and Jesus felt bad for them. Then Mary took Jesus aside and asked him to help their friends. She knew that Jesus can do anything and she hoped he would help. So Jesus went into the kitchen and asked a servant to bring in six jugs of water. (Pour water into the sandwich bags until each is half filled.) **When the water was brought into the kitchen, Jesus told the servant to pour some into a cup to take to the master of the party. The master couldn't believe his eyes. There was more wine, and it was the best he had ever tasted! Jesus had helped his friends in secret and performed his first miracle on earth!**

Sprinkle several spoonfuls of powdered grape soft-drink mix into each sandwich bag, then seal the bags tightly. Let kids gently mix the liquid and watch as it turns from clear to purple. Then open each bag a bit at the corner and slide in the drinking straw. Invite kids to sit around the edge of the shower curtain. Say: **As you sip your fruity drink, let's explore a bit more about the power of Jesus to do miracles and wondrous feats and where his power came from.**

MAKING IT MEMORABLE

Let kids sip their drinks and nibble on the plate of treats. Read aloud Matthew 28:18, then ask:

★ *What power and authority did God give to his Son?*
★ *Is there anything Jesus cannot do? Explain.*

Read aloud Philippians 3:20, 21. Then ask:

★ *What does Jesus have control of?*
★ *How does knowing that all things are possible with Jesus strengthen your faith?*

Read aloud Jude 25, then ask:

★ *For how long does Jesus' power and authority last?*
★ *How can we thank and praise Jesus for his power that was given by God?*

Say: **Jesus was given all power and authority from God the Father, and there is nothing that Jesus cannot do. Jesus has the power to help and heal in any way he chooses, from miracles to sending other people into our**

lives to help us. **With Jesus, all things are possible, and this amazing power and authority to control everything endures forever! What are we celebrating today? We're celebrating the fact that we love and serve such a perfect and powerful Lord!**

After kids have finished their treats, toss the drink bags in the trash. Then hand each child a balloon. Have kids use permanent markers to write the following rhyme on their balloons.

Jesus' power is perfect and true,
And there is nothing he can't do!

End by sharing a prayer thanking Jesus for using his power and authority to help and heal others. If there's time, close by singing "All Hail the Power" or "Awesome God."

Play a game of "Can You Do This?" Choose a child to be the first leader and have him challenge a friend by asking, "Can you do this?" Then the leader does a trick or action, such as hopping on one foot while patting his head. If the player who has been challenged can do the trick, she becomes the next leader. If the player cannot do the trick, she says, "I can't, but Jesus can do all things!" Then the leader challenges another player. Continue until all kids have been the leader.

CALMING STORMS

Jesus can calm our hearts and fears.

Psalms 27:1; 56:4; 91:2; Matthew 8:23-27; Hebrews 13:6

BEFORE BEGINNING...

Before beginning, gather the Story Kit items. Use masking tape to outline four simple boat shapes on the floor. Make sure the outlines are large enough for several kids to sit in and are at least 3 feet apart. Kids will be playing a game to get them focused on the Bible story, then will continue using the boats to help tell the story of Jesus calming the storm. In this story lesson, kids will discover that fear is normal but that trusting in Jesus is the one sure way to calm their hearts and worries.

Story Kit Supplies

❏ Bible
❏ masking tape

TELLING THE STORY

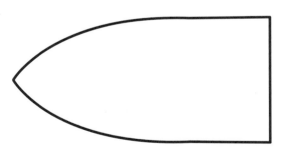

Make sure you've outlined the four boats on the floor using masking tape. Gather kids at one end of the room and explain that you'll play a game in which you'll call out a number from two to five. Kids will then rush to form the correct number of people and stand in the masking-tape boats. Then have kids re-form one group at the side of the room and call out another number. If any kids are left without a boat, tell them not to worry—they'll have another chance to play when you call out a new number.

After several turns, have kids form small groups and sit in the boats. Say: **It's a good thing our boats were on the floor and not water—especially since some of you missed the boat! Unlike Jesus' disciples one stormy night on the water, we didn't have to be afraid of drowning. Let's retell the exciting story of the time Jesus' disciples discovered that Jesus had power over nature and could calm the winds and seas just as he calmed their fears. You**

can help tell the story using your boats. **Follow along with the story actions and whenever you hear me say the word "boat," hop up and quickly climb into another boat before the story continues.**

Read the following story based on Matthew 8:23-27. Each time you say the "boat," pause for kids to respond by climbing into new boats and sitting down, then continue.

It had been a long day. Jesus had taught many crowds of people about God and his loving forgiveness. It was evening, and Jesus and his disciples were in a small, wooden fishing *boat*. (Pause.) **The disciples took turns rowing across the Sea of Galilee. Row with your pretend oars as we continue.**

Jesus was so tired from his teaching that he lay down for a nap. The *boat* glided across the water as Jesus slept. (Pause.) **The waves gently rocked Jesus back and forth as he slept. Rock back and forth in time to the waves.**

Suddenly, the wind came up, and the waves grew very big. They tossed the *boat* on the sea! (Pause.) **Jesus kept sleeping, but the disciples were afraid. Hold on to the sides so you don't fall overboard! The disciples thought the *boat* would sink.** (Pause.) **The storm grew even worse and the disciples even more scared. What could they do? They could wake Jesus! "Jesus! Help us!" they cried. Jesus woke up and stood at the front of the *boat*.** (Pause.)

Jesus commanded the wind, "Be still!"—and it did. Jesus ordered the waves, "Be calm!"—and they did! The wind and waves stopped at Jesus' command. Pause, then whisper: **The disciples were amazed. "Even the wind and waves obey him," they said. And they were no longer afraid.**

Say: **Wow! Jesus had ultimate control over the wind and waves, the sea and the storm! And the disciples understood that if Jesus has that kind of power from God, then what could they possibly be afraid of? Their trust, faith, and awe in Jesus grew a hundredfold that day. Let's explore more about Jesus' power to calm our fears, our worries, and our hearts.** Have kids stay in their four boats to look up a few Scripture verses.

MAKING IT MEMORABLE

Assign one of the following verses to each boat crew: Psalm 27:1; Psalm 56:4; Psalm 91:2; and Hebrews 13:6. Have crews read their verses and decide what the verse is teaching us about fear and faith in the Lord. After several minutes, invite each crew to read its verse and share what was learned with the whole class. Then ask:

★ *How are fear and faith connected in Jesus?*
★ *Why is it important to have faith instead of fear?*
★ *In what ways does Jesus calm our fears and the worries in our hearts?*

★ *Why do you think Jesus wants us to seek his help when we're afraid?*

Say: **The disciples in the boat turned to fear instead of faith, and Jesus rebuked them, saying they had little faith.** Read aloud Matthew 8:26, then continue: **Jesus wants us to have faith in his power instead of fear in situations or worries. Jesus knows we can love and serve him better when we are happy, calm, and unafraid. So the next time fear threatens to rock your boat, turn to faith instead of fear and ask Jesus to help!**

End by singing new words to the tune of "Row Your Boat" as kids row with pretend oars in the masking-tape boats. If kids are older and become familiar with the words, have them sing the lively song in a round.

> *Dread, tears, fright, and fears*
> *Will always rock the boat—*
> *Turn to faith instead of fear,*
> *And you will stay afloat!*

Make Calm My Fears paperweights by filling baby-food jars half full with water. Add several drops of blue food coloring and a teaspoon of clear glycerin (available at most pharmacies). In each jar, put a tiny sponge "boat" on the "sea," then glue the jar lid securely in place. Swirl and swish the jar to make waves on the sea. As the waters become still, pray and ask Jesus to calm whatever fears you may have. By the time the water is calm, your fears will be calmer, too!

WATER WALKIN'

We can follow Jesus by keeping our eyes on him!

Psalm 25:15; Matthew 14:22-33; Hebrews 12:2

BEFORE BEGINNING...

Story Kit Supplies

❑ **Bible**
❑ **paper plates**
❑ **index cards**
❑ **masking tape**

Before beginning, gather the Story Kit items as well as the following classroom supplies: markers. Be sure you have an index card and paper plate for each child. Before story time, tape paper plates to the floor in a large circle in the center of the room. Kids will be taping pictures of eyes to their backs and walking in a circle on the paper plates, keeping their eyes on the person in front of them. At the appointed time in the Bible story about Jesus walking on the water, kids will close their eyes and take ten steps, then open their eyes and see where they end up. With this demonstration, kids will learn that the only way to keep on a certain path is to keep their eyes open—and the only way to follow Jesus on the path to God is to keep their eyes on Jesus, as Peter should have done!

TELLING THE STORY

Make sure the paper plates are taped in a circle to the floor and that there's a paper plate for each person. Hand kids the index cards and markers and instruct them to draw a picture of eyeballs on one side of the cards. Then have kids help each other tape the cards to one another's backs. Explain that the paper plates are stepping-stones around a sea and that they'll be walking on them in a circle. Tell kids they must keep their eyes on the picture of the eyes in front of them, then say: **When we don't know where we're going or have anyone to trust and help us, life can be pretty scary—like walking a tightrope with your eyes closed. Jesus' friend, Peter, learned about keeping his eyes on Jesus one watery night. You can help tell our Bible story today by walking on our pretend stepping-stones and keeping your eyes on the eyes in front of you.**

Read the story below from Matthew 14:22-33 as kids walk from stepping-stone to stepping-stone around the circle. At the time indicated, have kids close their eyes and take ten more steps.

Jesus had been teaching people about God. When evening came, he told his disciples they could go on without him, so the disciples got into their boat to leave. Jesus stayed and prayed while the disciples sailed farther and farther from the shore. When they were quite a distance from the shore, the wind came upon the dark night. The disciples looked out on the water and saw a figure coming toward them. They were so afraid! What could it be? A ghost? Then a familiar voice said, "Don't be afraid; it is I." And the disciples saw Jesus. But Peter wasn't convinced. He said, "Lord, if it is really you, let me walk to you on the water." Peter got out of the boat. He looked at Jesus and started walking toward him on the water. But when the wind began to blow, Peter took his eyes away from Jesus and looked away. Close your eyes and take ten more steps as you count them aloud. Don't worry about bumping into someone—let's see where you end up!

After kids have taken ten steps, have them open their eyes and look around. Say: **Some of you look pretty watery and wet because you left the stepping-stones. It was easy to walk along when we had eyes open. But with them closed, it wasn't easy to keep from sinking into our pretend sea! That's what happened to Peter when he looked away from Jesus. Peter immediately began to sink. "Save me!" he cried, and Jesus reached out his hand to Peter and helped him back into the boat.** Have everyone get back on the steppingstones and begin walking in a circle again. **Jesus told Peter he had little faith. Then the wind stopped, and the disciples worshiped Jesus as the Son of God. They had seen amazing things that night! They saw Jesus' power to save through faith, and Peter had seen that the only way to follow Jesus is to keep our eyes on him all the time!**

Have kids sit on the paper plates. Say: **That is a real eye-opening story, isn't it? To follow Jesus and stay safe, we have to keep our eyes and faith on Jesus! Let's explore more about keeping our focus on Jesus.**

MAKING IT MEMORABLE

Invite volunteers to read aloud Psalms 25:15; 141:8a; and Hebrews 12:2. Then ask:

★ *Why is it important for us to keep our eyes on Jesus?*
★ *In what ways does having faith help up keep our eyes on Jesus and follow him better?*

Say: **When we keep our eyes on something or someone, it means we focus on them. Just as when we play a game of Follow the Leader, we must**

keep our eyes on Jesus as our heavenly leader to follow him the best we can. When we talk about keeping our eyes on Jesus, it means keeping our faith and trust focused on him—not our physical eyes. We must see Jesus with our hearts, minds, spirits, and especially our faith! Now let's walk around the stepping-stone circle as we share a prayer asking for Jesus' help in keeping our faith focused on him.

Share a prayer asking Jesus to help you keep your sights and faith trained on him alone. Then have kids use markers to write Hebrews 12:2 on their index cards. If there's time, sing "Jesus Loves Me."

Play a game of Keep Your Eyes on the Prize. Place the Story Kit on the floor behind a table and let a child choose six or seven of the items to line up on the table. Let the kids look at the items, then turn and look away while one of the items is taken away or another one is added. Then let kids try to identify what's missing or has been added. If the guess is correct, that child may be the next to choose items. End by reminding kids that the real prize is following Jesus and that the only way to follow him is by keeping our eyes and faith on him.

THANK YOU, JESUS

It's important to have a thankful spirit.

Psalm 100; Luke 17:11-19; 1 Thessalonians 5:18

BEFORE BEGINNING...

Before beginning, gather the Story Kit items as well as the following classroom supplies: scissors, paper towels, thin tempera or watercolor paint, brushes (or cotton swabs), and a bowl of soapy water. Choose light-colored paints such as pastels or white (if your shower curtain is a solid color and white will show up on it). Cut 12-inch pieces of white shelf paper, one piece per child. Kids will be painting splotches on the shower curtain to represent the marks and spots on the ten lepers. Then, as the story unfolds, kids will use the soapy water and paper towels (or sponges) to remove the spots. In this story lesson, kids will discover that it's important to have a thankful spirit and to be willing and anxious to express our thanks to Jesus for his loving help. Kids will end the lesson by painting thank-you cards for Jesus on white shelf paper.

Story Kit Supplies

❏ Bible
❏ plastic shower curtain
❏ cookie sheet
❏ shelf paper
❏ newspapers

TELLING THE STORY

Spread the plastic shower curtain on the floor and place the paints and soapy water on the cookie sheet in the center of the curtain. (Place newspapers under the shower curtain for extra protection against spills.) Hand each child a paintbrush or cotton swab and have kids find places to sit around the edge of the shower curtain. Say: **Think for a moment—if you could paint a picture to thank Jesus for his love and help, what designs would you include? A heart to express your love or perhaps a bright sun to express the warmth you feel for him? There are so many ways to express our thanks to Jesus for all he is and all he does. After all, it's only natural to want to thank Jesus, right? But once long ago, a group of people weren't so thankful or grateful. We'll use these paints and this shower curtain to retell the story**

of ten men who needed Jesus and his help and how only one of the men had a thankful heart.

Retell the story of the ten lepers from Luke 17:11-19. Have kids paint characters and splotches at the appropriate times during the story. Remind kids to be careful not to smudge or smear paint on themselves.

Once there were ten lepers. Leprosy was a terrible disease. It was a very ugly and painful skin disease that made sores and splotches and blotches all over a person's body. (Have kids each paint three spots on the shower curtain.) **No one liked people with leprosy very much. People were afraid they'd catch the disease, so they kept people with leprosy away. Imagine how lonely the sick people must have felt!** (Have kids each paint a small, sad face on the curtain.) **Even though most people were afraid of lepers, Jesus wasn't. Jesus loved all people equally. One day, Jesus met ten lepers on the road. The lepers stayed back from Jesus but called, "Please have pity on us, Lord!"**

Do you know what Jesus did? He took away their sore spots and cleansed them! (Have kids silently and quickly wash away the spots and sad faces using soapy water and paper towels.) **Imagine how happy those ten men were!** (Have each person paint a happy face on the curtain.) **Nine of the men ran to tell their friends they had been healed. They didn't stop to even say thank you to Jesus! How rude and ungrateful they were! But one man did something different. One man came back to thank Jesus and praise God!** (Paint hearts on the shower curtain.) **Only one man expressed his thanks and love to Jesus for his amazing gift of healing. But that man knew that Jesus is pleased when we have a thankful spirit and express our thanks to the Lord!** (Write the words "Thank you" on the shower curtain.)

Set aside the painting supplies, then step back from the shower curtain to let it dry. Say: **Imagine not even bothering to thank Jesus for his miraculous, loving help! We know that expressing our thanks to Jesus and God honors and worships the Lord, and that is one reason we come to church. Let's explore more about expressing our thanks and gratitude for Jesus' love, mercy, and help.** Slide the shower curtain away from the newspapers and let it dry. You'll be painting on the newspapers in a few minutes, so leave them in place.

MAKING IT MEMORABLE

Invite volunteers to read aloud 1 Chronicles 16:8, 34; Psalm 7:17; and 1 Thessalonians 5:18. Then ask:

★ *Why do you think Jesus wanted to help the lepers? Why does he want to help us?*

★ *In what ways does expressing our thanks for Jesus demonstrate our love for him?*

★ *What are things you can thank Jesus for?*
★ *In what different ways can we express our thanks?*

Say: **There are so many ways to express our love and thanks to Jesus! One way is by reading God's Word. Let's read a psalm of thanksgiving together for Jesus.** Read aloud, in unison, Psalm 100. Then invite kids to paint thank-you cards or posters for Jesus using shelf paper and the paints. If there's time, hang the shower curtain in the room so kids can be reminded of the importance of thanking Jesus each day for all he does. (The paints will wash off with warm soapy water when you're ready to clean the shower curtain and return it to the Story Kit.) End by singing "What a Friend We Have in Jesus" if there's time.

Get the wiggles out by playing a quick thank-you relay. Let kids each choose a resource item from the Story Kit. Then form two or three relay lines and place all the resource items from each team in front of the first person in each line. When you say "go," have the first person in each line pass an item to the person behind him and say "thank you." Continue passing and thanking until all items reach the backs of the lines and travel forward again.

GONE FISHING

God provides for our every need.

Matthew 7:7-11, 17:24-27; Philippians 4:19

BEFORE BEGINNING...

Before beginning, gather the Story Kit items as well as the following classroom supplies: construction paper, tape, and scissors. Since this is a Wow 'Em Bible story, you'll also need toothpicks and a fresh bakery hard roll and shiny quarter for each child. You'll be hiding a coin in each roll before this devotion, so make sure the coins are washed in hot soapy water and dried. (Kids will not know the coins are inside!) Cut circles of blue construction paper and place them on the paper plates to represent water. Then hold each roll

Story Kit Supplies

❏ **Bible**
❏ **paper plates**
❏ **index cards**

in both hands and press your thumbs carefully into the bottom of the roll to make a small opening. Slide a quarter into the center of the roll. Prepare a roll and hidden quarter for each child and place the rolls on the plates before beginning the story lesson. Kids will be making their rolls look like fish during the Bible story about the time Jesus needed tax money for the collectors and told Peter to take the first fish caught from the lake and open it to find a silver coin. In this fun story lesson, kids will actually open their fishy rolls to discover the treasure hidden within! Then as they nibble their treats, kids will discover that God always provides for their needs, just as he did for Jesus. (Note: Kids can add their quarters to the collection plate, or for a more memorable effect, let kids take their treasures home! They'll be excited to show everyone the shiny quarter they got in class and will certainly be asked to tell about how they received it.)

TELLING THE STORY

Set out index cards, toothpicks, construction paper, and scissors. Have kids sit on the floor or at a table and hand each person a plate with a roll sitting on the blue paper water. Tell kids not to pick up their rolls yet—that will come later. Say: **Don't these rolls look almost like fish floating in the sea? Fish are mentioned** many times in the Bible, but one of my favorite fishy stories happened in the New Testament. As we tell the story of how Jesus needed something that God provided, we'll turn your rolls into fish by adding paper fins. When it's time, you can quickly cut or tear a back fin from colored paper or index cards. Tape the fin on a toothpick, then stick it in your roll. We'll make a back fin and a tail fin. As you listen to the story, listen carefully for what Jesus and Peter needed and how God provided it through Jesus' power.

Peter came to Jesus one day and told Jesus that the tax collectors were wanting their taxes. Unfortunately, Peter didn't have any money to give. "What shall we do?" wondered Peter. Jesus wasn't worried. "Go to the lake," he told Peter, "and when you catch the first fish, open its mouth." Quickly make your back fin as we answer a couple of questions. Remind kids to keep their fish on the plates and not to pick them up as they work.

As kids work on their back fins, ask:

★ *Why do you think Jesus wasn't worried about how they would pay the taxes?*

★ *Why was it good that Peter told Jesus what they needed?*

After the back fins are stuck in place on top of the rolls, continue the story: **Peter obeyed Jesus and went to the lake. The first fish he caught was wiggly, but he managed to open its mouth. Quickly make your tail fins as we answer a couple of questions.** As kids work on the tail fins, ask:

★ *In what ways did Peter obey Jesus?*

★ *Why is it important to obey after we've asked for Jesus' help when we need something?*

After the tail fins are stuck in place at the backs of the rolls, continue the story. Say: **When Peter opened the fish's mouth, what do you suppose he found? Peter found a four-drachma coin—a silver coin that was just enough to pay their taxes! Imagine that—Jesus knew a coin would be found in the fish's mouth, and it was just what they needed! In a moment, we'll open your fish to see what you might find. But first, let's answer a few more story questions and read a bit more about how God provides for us.**

MAKING IT MEMORABLE

Invite volunteers to read aloud Matthew 7:7-11 and Philippians 4:19. Then ask:

★ *Why do you think God wants us to ask for what we need?*

★ *In what ways does asking God for our needs keep us humble and not prideful?*

★ *Why does God want to provide what we need?*

★ *How does God show his love in providing for our needs through Jesus?*

Say: **Jesus wasn't worried about the taxes because he knew their needs would be powerfully provided through God's power. Jesus wanted Peter to realize that he could provide for their needs—but what an unusual way Jesus provided the coin! Now you can open your fishy rolls and see if you find anything inside!**

After kids discover their hidden coins, let them eat their rolls as you chat about ways God provides for us, such as through giving us courage when we're afraid, supplying food and shelter when we need it, and by offering us forgiveness and eternal life through Jesus. End with a prayer thanking Jesus for meeting our needs and for giving us all we need when we humbly ask him.

If there's time, sing the following song to the tune of "If You're Happy and You Know It."

If you're thankful and you know it, clap your hands!
If you're thankful and you know it, clap your hands!
If you're thankful and you know it, then your prayers will surely show it.
If you're thankful and you know it, clap your hands!

Let God use your class to help provide for someone else's needs. Have kids make a fishy fruit basket for an elderly church member by cutting out paper fins and taping them to fresh fruits such as apples, bananas, oranges, lemons (for tea), and pears. Place your fish in the netting from a fruit bag so it looks like a great catch of fish. Then copy the words to the song above on one side of an index card and let kids sign their first names to the back of the card. (For a whimsical touch, toss in a bag of candy worms!)

KINDNESS COUNTS

Jesus taught us to be compassionate to all people.

Luke 10:25-37; 2 Corinthians 1:3; Colossians 3:12

BEFORE BEGINNING...

Before beginning, gather the Story Kit items. Kids will be using Story Kit props to act out the story of the Good Samaritan and how he showed kindness and compassion to the may who lay hurt in the road. The story presentation is simple as kids explore ways Jesus showed compassion to others and why it's important for us to express our love for Jesus and other people through the kindness and compassion in our hearts.

Story Kit Supplies

❏ **Bible**
❏ **3 dish towels**
❏ **newspapers**
❏ **3 men's neckties**
❏ **plastic spoons**
❏ **5 plastic coins**

TELLING THE STORY

Gather kids and explain that you'll begin by role playing a few situations and what kids might do in them. Have pairs or trios come forward to act out the following situations and what they would do in each.

★ *You and a couple of friends are walking to school when your friend trips and falls. What do you do?*

★ *The kid at school who is mean to everyone drops his lunch in a puddle before school. What do you do?*

★ *You and your friends are playing ball near a cranky neighbor's house. The ball goes into his yard, which happens to need raking badly. What do you do when he comes out to scold you?*

After acting out the situations and what kids would do, say: **It's pretty easy to be kind and compassionate to our friends or people who are nice to us. But it's not always easy to care about someone who's mean to us or to people we don't know well. But Jesus was kind and compassionate to all people and wants us to be the same. Having compassion means putting ourselves in someone else's shoes and feeling what they feel. It was so important for us to learn about kindness that Jesus told a parable, or story, about a man who went out of his way to help a stranger when no one else would. Since**

you've already warmed up with a bit of acting, I'll need seven volunteers to play the roles in this Bible story. The rest of you can be members of the sound machine and make story sound effects.

Choose three kids to wear dish towels on their heads and have them tie neckties around their foreheads to keep the towels in place. Assign one person to be the Levite, one to play the priest, and the other to be the Good Samaritan. A fourth child can hold the five plastic coins and be the man who gets hurt. Three volunteers will be robbers who throw newspaper wads at the man they are robbing. The rest of the class can make sound effects. Rub newspapers or tap plastic spoons together to make the sound of footsteps walking along the road; clap hands on knees to make running sounds; and click tongues to make the clopping of donkey hooves. Narrate the following story from Luke 10:25-37 as kids act and sound out their parts.

One day, a Jewish man was walking along a road carrying his money in his hand. (Have "hurt man" walk along carrying the five coins. The sound machine can make the rustling of footsteps.) **Suddenly, three robbers jumped out at the man. They hurt and robbed the poor man!** (Have the robbers toss their paper stones at the hurt man and take his coins.) **The rotten robbers ran away and left the man hurt and lying on the side of the road.** (Have the hurt man lie on the floor while the robbers run away. The sound machine can make the noise of running footsteps.)

The hurt man lay there quite a while, but then he heard someone walking down the road and saw a priest coming. (Have the sound machine make walking sounds as the priest approaches the hurt man.) **"Surely he will help me," thought the hurt man. But did he? No, he didn't. The priest passed by the hurt man and kept on walking!** (Have the priest pass by the hurt man.) **Then the hurt man heard more footsteps coming. It was a Levite. "Surely he will help me," thought the hurt man. But did he? No, he didn't. The Levite passed by the hurt man and kept on walking!** (Have the Levite pass by the hurt man.) **Then the poor man heard clip-clip-clopping coming near.** (Have the sound machine make trotting sounds.) **"Oh, no," thought the hurt man, when he saw it was a man from Samaria. "He'll never stop. He is a Samaritan, and we don't like each other. If the priest and Levite wouldn't stop to help me, he certainly won't!" But did the Samaritan stop? Yes!** (Have the Good Samaritan stop and kneel by the hurt man and pretend to bandage him up.) **The Good Samaritan cleaned the hurt man's wounds and took him to town on his donkey. Then he paid money for someone to care for the hurt man and make him well. The Samaritan had been the only one who was good and kind to the hurt man—even though they had not been friends! Let's clap for the Good Samaritan—and for showing compassion to all people!** Lead children in a round of lively clapping.

Say: **The Good Samaritan was the only one to stop and show compassion to the hurt man—even when they were not supposed to be friends. Let's explore more about showing compassion even when it's not easy and why Jesus wants us to be kind to all people.** Set aside the Story Kit items.

MAKING IT MEMORABLE

Gather kids and say: **Jesus showed us about compassion throughout his entire life. We read of so many times Jesus had compassion for the sick, helpless, hungry, and weak. Let's read about times Jesus showed compassion and kindness to others.** Invite volunteers to read aloud the following verses: Matthew 9:36; 14:14; 15:32; 20:34; and Mark 1:40, 41. Then ask:

★ *How is having compassion a way to express love for others? Jesus?*
★ *Why do you think Jesus had such great compassion for others?*

Read aloud 2 Corinthians 1:3; Ephesians 4:32; and Colossians 3:12. Then ask:

★ *How does it feel to help a friend? to help someone you don't know?*
★ *How are compassion, kindness, patience, and mercy related?*
★ *In what ways can you show kindness to someone today?*

Say: **The man from Samaria had great compassion on the man lying in the road, even though he wasn't supposed to like him. But the man had such love in his heart that he was willing to stop and help the man with compassion, kindness, patience, and mercy. This is exactly what Jesus did his whole life and just how Jesus wants us to be!** Sing the following words based on Ephesians 4:32 to the tune of "Ten Little Indians."

> *Be kind and loving to one another;*
> *Be forgiving of each other,*
> *Just as in Christ God forgave you.*
> *Ephesians 4:32.*

Use white shelf paper and let kids create a kindness collage. Provide a 3-foot length of white shelf paper from the Story Kit, markers, crayons, and a variety of self-adhesive bandages. Let kids stick the bandages to the paper and use markers and crayons to decorate them. Then write the following verse across the top of the collage: *"Love your enemies and pray for those who persecute you." Matthew 5:44.* Use markers to write other verses about kindness and compassion on the paper, including Colossians 3:12 and 2 Corinthians 1:3. Hang your display in a place where others can enjoy and read the important reminders of being kind and compassionate to others.

BUILDING BASES

Jesus is the foundation we build our lives on.

Matthew 7:24-27; 1 Corinthians 3:10, 11; 2 Timothy 2:19

BEFORE BEGINNING...

Before beginning, gather the Story Kit items. In this lesson about Jesus' parable of the wise and foolish builders, kids will work together to build a foundation using index cards, much like building a playing-card house. One base will be the Bible. One base will be the index cards. Then you'll place a coin on top of each foundation and kids will put the structures to the great foundation test by blowing hard on the both bases. In this lesson, kids will learn that it's important to build our lives on the rock-solid foundation of Jesus.

Story Kit Supplies

❑ **Bible**
❑ **index cards**
❑ **2 plastic coins**

TELLING THE STORY

Form groups of four or five and hand each person five index cards. Explain that kids will use the index cards during the Bible story to build bases or foundations much like card houses. Then ask kids if they've ever built anything, such as a birdhouse, doghouse, toy race car, or any other structure. Encourage kids to tell what they used for building materials and why they chose those materials.

Then say: **It's fun to build things, but what we choose to build them from is very important. If we use flimsy or broken materials, our project will probably fall apart. Jesus knew the value of building with solid materials, and he wanted to teach us about building, too. So Jesus told a parable, or story, about a wise builder and a foolish builder. As we listen to the Bible story, you can be building in your group, too. Each time you hear me say the word "build," add a card to your group's structure, just as if you're building a card house. You'll be making a base or foundation on which we'll set a pretend house later.**

Retell the parable of the wise and foolish builders from Matthew 7:24-27, pausing for kids to add cards when you say the word "build."

Once there were two men who wanted to *build* **houses.** (Pause to add cards.) **One man was wise, and the other was foolish. The foolish man decided to** *build* **his house on the sand.** (Pause to add cards.) **The wise man chose to** *build* **his house on solid rock.** (Pause to add cards.) **What do you suppose happened when the strong winds and rains came? The rains came up and made the sand soggy, and before you knew it, the house on the sand was swept away! But when the waters came upon the house on solid rock, it stood still and didn't get washed away. When we** *build* **on weak bases or foundations** (pause to add cards), **they can't withstand troubles. But when we** *build* **on strong bases or foundations** (pause to add cards), **no troubles can destroy what's been built!**

When the cards are used up, say: **Wow! I see a lot of foundations that have been built here, but there's one more we want to add.** Set the Bible on the floor by the card foundations. **Now let's give our bases or foundations the ol' stress test. We'll set these pretend houses on the first two foundations and blow on the bases to see what happens.** Place the plastic coins on two different foundations made of index cards, then have kids kneel down to blow on the cards.

After the cards blow down and the coins fall, try two more and so on until all of the card foundations are flat on the floor. Say: **I guess these foundations couldn't hold up under troubles, just like the house on the sand. But what about our other foundation? Let's give it the stress test!**

Place a coin on top of the Bible, then have kids blow on the Bible to try and collapse it. Say: **This strong foundation stood the test and stayed safe and firm— just like the house built on the rock-solid foundation!** Ask:

★ *Why is where we choose to build important?*
★ *In what ways is building our lives on Jesus like building houses on a strong and sturdy foundation?*

Say: **Jesus told this parable so we would recognize where to build our lives—on him! Jesus is the only rock-solid place on which to build our lives and faith. Let's explore more about building our lives and faith on Jesus and why he is so rock solid.**

MAKING IT MEMORABLE

Read aloud 1 Corinthians 3:10, 11 and ask:

★ *Why is Jesus our perfect foundation, strong and unbreakable?*
★ *How can we make Jesus our foundation in life?*
★ *How does relying on Jesus' truth and strength help us make our foundation even stronger?*

Read aloud 2 Timothy 2:19, then ask:

★ *How does being God's children help us develop a strong foundation in the Lord?*

★ *In what ways does turning from evil and embracing God strengthen our foundation in the Lord?*

Say: **Laying a firm foundation for our lives means learning God's truth through reading, understanding, and using his Word. It means relying on Jesus to help us when we ask for his help. It means talking to God through prayer and worship. And it means pushing away anything that would try to become our foundation, such as money, lies, or evil. It's only through having built our lives on the strong and perfect foundation of Jesus Christ that we will stand firm and unshaken no matter what may come our way!**

Let's thank Jesus for being our firm foundation and for helping us build our lives in him alone. Share a prayer thanking Jesus, then sing "The Rains Came Down and the Floods Came Up" as you act out the motions.

Have each child make a nifty house-in-a-jar as a reminder of the wise and foolish builders and how Jesus wants us to build our lives and faith on him alone. For each jar, you'll need tacky craft glue, water, glitter, a clean baby-food jar and lid, a rock just large enough to fit inside the jar, florist's clay, and small houses from an old Monopoly game. Use florist's clay to stick the rock to the bottom of the jar, then use another small ball of clay to stick the house to the top of the rock. Fill the jar three-quarters full of water and add a half teaspoon of glitter. Glue around the inside rim of the lid and screw the lid on tightly. Let the jar dry for twenty-four hours before shaking it.

SEEKING THE LOST

Each one of us is precious in God's kingdom.

Luke 15:3-10; 19:10; James 4:8

BEFORE BEGINNING...

Before beginning, gather the Story Kit items. Before class, hide the plastic coin and the picture of the sheep from the Story Kit somewhere in the room. Hide the items in places challenging enough for older kids to enjoy but not frustrating for younger kids. Suspend the shower curtain or hang it over a table tipped sideways to make a place for kids to hide. Kids will play a simple game to introduce the story lesson, then form two groups to hunt and find the plastic coin and picture of the sheep. In this story lesson based on Jesus' parables of the lost sheep and coin, kids will discover the importance of "one" and why each of us is special and precious to God. The More Fun activity is very easy but reinforces the point that each one of us is important.

Story Kit Supplies

❏ Bible
❏ plastic shower curtain
❏ 1 plastic coin
❏ Picture Prop (sheep)

TELLING THE STORY

Be sure the plastic shower curtain is positioned so kids can hide behind it. Also, make certain that the plastic coin and picture of the sheep are hidden in the room for kids to find later.

Gather kids in a group by the shower curtain. that Explain you'll play a game to see how observant everyone is. Have kids hide their eyes, then tap someone's head. The person chosen will tiptoe behind the shower curtain, after which the rest of the kids can take turns guessing who is missing. Whoever guesses correctly may choose the next person to hide. Continue for several turns, then say: **It's fun to pretend we're hiding or to guess who might be missing from a group. But when we become lost from God or wander away from his truth and love, it's no game. Each of us is important to the Lord, and he wants no one to be lost or missing from him. Jesus told two parables, or stories, about being lost. One parable was about a shepherd who had a lost sheep, and the**

other was about a woman who lost a coin. Let's form two groups to help with the stories. Have kids form two groups: one will be the Lambs and one the Coins. Say: I'll tell both parables, then you'll have a chance to search for our own missing sheep and coin in the room.

A shepherd had one hundred sheep, but one day one of his precious sheep was missing. Instead of saying, "I'm not looking—what a bore! One may be lost, but I still have more," the shepherd searched and hunted until the lost lamb was found—and he was so happy that he called his friends to celebrate that his lost sheep had been found.

Now there was a woman who was much like the shepherd. She had ten coins she greatly treasured, but one day one of her precious coins was missing. Instead of saying, "I'm not looking—what a bore! One may be lost, but I still have more," the woman searched her whole house top to bottom until the coin was finally found. She was so happy that she called her friends to celebrate that her lost coin had been found.

Say: There is a lost sheep and a lost coin somewhere in this room. When I say "go," you may search for your group's missing item. If you happen to see the other group's item, don't say a word! When your group's item is found, your group must all shout, "What was lost is found!" and give each other high fives. When both items are found, we'll explore a bit more about the way God treasures us.

MAKING IT MEMORABLE

After the items have been found, gather kids and say: Jesus told the parables of the lost sheep and coin to show that, just as the lamb and coin were important to the shepherd and woman, we're important to God. Ask:
★ *Why did the shepherd and woman search for their lost sheep and coin when they had others?*
★ *Does Jesus love each of us or only some of us? Explain.*
★ *Why is each "one" precious to God? In other words, he has a whole world full of people—can each person be precious to him?*
Invite volunteers to read aloud Luke 15:10; 19:10; and James 4:8a. Then ask:
★ *How does sin draw us away from God and make us lost?*

★ *Why does God and all of heaven rejoice when a person lost in sin is found and forgiven?*

★ *In what way does drawing near to God help us keep from becoming lost?*

★ *How can you help others when they become "lost" from Jesus?*

Say: **Jesus wanted us to know that God loves each of us and embraces every one of us in his heart. God wants us to stay close to him and not wander away and become lost in sin. That's why the Lord seeks to bring us back if we wander from him. But the best way to keep from becoming lost from God is to stay close to him through prayer, reading the Bible, serving him, and being kind to others! Let's share a prayer thanking Jesus for loving each one of us and for helping us stay "found" in God's heart!**

Share a prayer, then close by singing "Amazing Grace."

Bring in sugar, unsweetened soft-drink mix, a pitcher of water, a large spoon, and small paper cups. Set the sugar aside and mix just the unsweetened drink mix into 2 quarts of cold water. Ask for a taste tester to sample your fruity drink. When your taster says it tastes bitter or sour, ask kids why one little ingredient such as sugar could really matter so much. Then add the amount of sugar indicated on the drink mix package and let kids sip their treats. Remind kids that, just as one little ingredient was vital to the drink, each one of them is important to God and his kingdom.

TALL LOVE

Love and forgiveness can change lives.

Luke 19:1-10; John 13:34; Ephesians 4:32

BEFORE BEGINNING...

Story Kit Supplies

- ❏ **Bible**
- ❏ **newspapers**

Before beginning, gather the Story Kit items as well as green construction paper, scissors, tape, markers, and copies of the verses from page 112, one for each child. (If you prefer, kids can write the verses.) Practice making a tree from newspapers so you can guide kids to make their own. To make a tree trunk, lay a sheet of newspaper flat and begin rolling it from the bottom until it's about 2 inches from the top edge. Place another sheet of newspaper over the top edge of the first sheet, overlapping the two papers. Continue rolling the paper, then add another sheet of paper. Keep rolling and adding more papers four more times. Roll the last sheet of paper all the way up so that you have a long, thin tube. Securely tape the paper at each end of the paper tube. Make five 4-inch cuts on the top end of the tube to make the fronds of the tree. Now pull the inside layers at the bottom of the tube outward or downward to make the tube "grow." When the tube is about 5 feet tall, you'll have a tremendous tree! Tear green construction-paper leaves and tape them to the top fringe. Kids will make and elongate paper trees during the story. Later kids will tear paper leaves, write verses on them, then tape the leaves to the tops of their trees. This story lesson about Zacchaeus will help kids realize that loving Jesus and receiving his forgiveness changes our lives in wonderful ways.

TELLING THE STORY

Set out the newspapers, scissors, and tape. Ask kids what the phrase "life-changing" means. Allow several responses, then say: **The phrase *life-changing* refers to something or someone who makes such great changes in our hearts and minds that we change the way we live. In other words, there are changes on the inside of us that come out on the outside in how we treat others and the way we speak. Life-changes can be good or bad, but when that life-change is made by Jesus, it's awesome! A life changed by Jesus is a life that becomes**

filled with hope, love, and faith. And that's just what the guy in today's story discovered the day Jesus came to his town. Let's make a story prop to help tell this neat Bible story. Watch carefully and follow me!

Show kids how to make the rolled newspapers, but only *begin* to lengthen them. Then say: **Each time you hear the word "tall," pull out a bit more of your newspaper roll to lengthen it. And each time you hear the word "small," squat down low on the floor to make yourself very short.**

Long ago lived a man named Zacchaeus. He was a short, *small* man who wasn't liked by anyone, because Zacchaeus was a tax collector who took the people's money and kept a lot for himself. Zacchaeus wasn't friendly at all, and it would have been a *tall* order for him to stop being mean, because he had a very *small* heart! One day, Jesus was coming to town, and everyone was excited to see him—even Zacchaeus. But there was a big problem. Zacchaeus was so *small* that he couldn't see over the crowd. How could he become *tall?* Then Zacchaeus saw a *tall* tree standing along the road. So Zacchaeus climbed the tree and went from short and *small* to very, very *tall!*

As Jesus walked by, Zacchaeus peeked down. Jesus stopped under the tree. "Zacchaeus," said Jesus, "Come down. We'll go to your house today." Zacchaeus was so surprised he wasn't sure what to do . Then he scampered down that *tall* tree and headed for his home with Jesus. When Zacchaeus and Jesus shared supper in the *small* kitchen, the people in the town complained and felt their hearts grow *small*. "Why should Jesus eat with him?" they griped. "He is a very bad man, and no one likes him!"

But Jesus had *tall* plans for Zacchaeus! Jesus forgave Zacchaeus for the wrong things he had done and showed Zacchaeus kindness and compassion. Wow! In that moment, Zacchaeus's heart went from *small* to very, very *tall!* Jesus' love, acceptance, and forgiveness changed Zacchaeus's life forever! How do we know? Because everyone could see the changes in Zacchaeus's life when he gave back all the money he had stolen—and even more! His heart had changed from stingy and *small* to warm and *tall!*

Have kids hold up their tree trunks, which should be long by now. Say: **Jesus loved and forgave Zacchaeus, and he wants us to love others and forgive them, too—no matter who they are or what they've done. Love can be life-changing, and when a life is changed to love and serve Jesus, it's also a life saved! Let's explore more about the power of love and forgiveness to work miracles in people's lives. We'll use our tree trunks to help.**

MAKING IT MEMORABLE

Hand kids green construction paper and have them each tear six paper leaves. Make the leaves about 4 inches long and 3 inches wide. Have markers ready. If you photocopied the verse cards on page 112, be sure each child has a copy of the three verses. If you did not copy the cards, kids can use markers to write the verses on their paper leaves.

Read aloud John 13:34, then have kids either cut and tape the verse cards on their paper leaves or write the verse on their leaves. After the verse is in place, ask:

★ *How did Jesus' love change Zacchaeus's life?*

★ *How has your life changed after loving Jesus?*

Read aloud 2 Corinthians 5:17, then have kids attach or write the verse on another of their leaves. Ask:

★ *How did Zacchaeus's life become changed and new after meeting Jesus?*

★ *What changes in our lives when we accept Jesus' love and forgiveness?*

Read aloud Ephesians 4:32, then have kids attach or write the verse on another of their leaves. Ask:

★ *How does feeling loved and accepted help you reach out to others? serve Jesus?*

★ *How can sharing Jesus with someone change that person's life?*

★ *In what ways can you show someone you accept him or her this week?*

Have kids write words that show how we can treat others as Jesus did, such as through kindness, love, forgiveness, compassion, and acceptance. Then tape all six leaves to the paper fringes on the tops of the paper tree trunks.

Say: **Jesus taught us that loving and forgiving others as he did can change other's lives in miraculous ways. And Jesus wants us to know that, just as Zacchaeus was changed for the better, we can help change lives by sharing Jesus' love and forgiveness. Think of someone you can accept and be kind to this week, then go for it! We can change lives for Jesus—one life at a time!** If there's time, sing "Zacchaeus Was a Wee Little Man" as you act out the motions.

Play a coin-toss game to remind kids how Zacchaeus gave back the people's coins when his life was changed by Jesus. Form kids into two rows facing each other about a foot apart. Hand one team the five coins from the Story Kit. When you call out "coin catch!" have the kids holding coins toss them to people in the other line. If a coin is dropped, the child who tossed it joins the other team. After the coins have been tossed, have teams each take a step backward. Continue tossing, catching, and stepping until everyone is on one team.

HOSANNA, JESUS!

We can welcome Jesus into our lives each day.

Matthew 21:1-9; John 5:23; Revelation 3:20; 5:12

BEFORE BEGINNING...

Before beginning, gather the Story Kit items as well as scissors, a stapler, markers, and green construction paper. Cut a 10-inch length of ribbon for each child and place the ribbons into pocket #3. Cut a small palm leaf from green construction paper and snip the edges to fringe it. Slide the leaf into pocket #6 of the Story Apron. Put the picture of Jesus into pocket #1, the picture of the donkey into pocket #2, the coins into pocket #4, the jingle bell into pocket #5, and the picture of the heart into pocket #7. Kids will reveal items from the Story Apron as you retell the story of Jesus' triumphal entry into Jerusalem. This story lesson will teach kids that the greatest gift we can give to honor Jesus is our love. Be sure you have enough green construction paper for kids to make their own 6-inch palm fronds. They'll be stapling the ribbon to the fronds to wave during a closing song.

Story Kit Supplies

❑ **Bible**
❑ **Story Apron**
❑ **1 jingle bell**
❑ **ribbon**
❑ **2 plastic coins**
❑ **Picture Props (Jesus, heart, donkey)**

TELLING THE STORY

Tie the Story Apron around your waist and gather kids in a group. Ask:

★ ***What's the most special, precious, lasting gift you could give someone? Why?***

Say: **Long ago, Jesus came to Jerusalem for the last time. Soon he would die for us on the cross. The people of Jerusalem who had followed Jesus were very excited! They knew he was approaching and wanted to honor him in the best ways they could. But what could they do to honor him? Let's see what the people did for Jesus to welcome him into Jerusalem. We'll use the Story Apron to help.** Invite volunteers to pull pictures and items out of the pockets on the apron when it's time. Hand each child a ribbon when you reveal pocket #3.

What excitement there was in the city of Jerusalem! Jesus was coming, and everyone wanted to see him (pocket #1). **Jesus would come riding on a donkey** (pocket #2) **and go right in front of the crowds along the road. The people wanted to welcome Jesus in a special way that would honor him. But what could they do that was special enough? How could they welcome Jesus in just the right way?**

They might buy him a gift wrapped up with a bow (pocket #3)
Or present him with lilies as white as the snow.
They could give them their money all shiny and bright, (pocket #4)
But somehow the coins just didn't seem quite right.
What about music to brighten the day— (pocket #5)
Would that say all that they wanted to say?
Then the people knew what they would wave
To honor dear Jesus and give him the praise.
They'd wave palm branches as green as could be (pocket #6)
To show that Jesus was their victory! (Have kids wave their ribbons.)
"Hosanna, blessed is he who comes in the name of the Lord!"
The people sang the praises as they never had before!
And when they waved the palm branches high above,
They gave Jesus the gift of their honor and love! (pocket #7)
And just as the people welcomed Jesus that day,
We can welcome him into our lives the same way!

Have kids wave their ribbons once more as you lead them in saying, "Hosanna, hosanna! Blessed is he who comes in the name of the Lord!" Set down the ribbons and say: **Wow! What a truly triumphant entry into Jerusalem. Jesus knew he was coming to die in a few days, yet he chose to come anyway. Jesus rode into the city in victory because he knew he was bringing us victory over sin and eternal death. The people didn't know all of this, but they loved him and honored him by waving palm branches and laying their robes at his feet for the donkey to walk on. Let's learn more about how we can welcome Jesus into our lives and praise him as these people did.**

MAKING IT MEMORABLE

Hand out green construction paper. Gather kids and read aloud John 5:23b, which teaches about honoring God and the Son. Then ask:

★ *How does loving God mean we love and accept Jesus, too?*
★ *If we don't welcome Jesus into our hearts and lives, is it possible to welcome and honor God? Explain.*

Say: **If we honor and praise Jesus and welcome him into our lives, then we also welcome, honor, and love God, our heavenly Father. It makes sense,** doesn't it? After all, how can we love and honor one without the other? **The green paper you have is the color of evergreen, which represents the ever-growing love we have for both God and his Son. Tear a large paper leaf from the green paper.** After the leaves are torn, have kids use markers to write "Love God and the Son!" on the leaves.

Read aloud Revelation 3:20 and 5:12, then ask:

★ *If Jesus was standing at your door knocking, would you answer and welcome him inside your home? Why?*

★ *How is this like welcoming Jesus into our hearts and lives?*

★ *Why is Jesus worthy to be praised and honored?*

★ *What are ways you can honor and praise Jesus today?*

Say: **Jesus wants us to welcome him into our hearts and lives as the main focus of our faith each day! Jesus wants to be welcomed warmly, and he is worthy to be praised and honored in all we do and say. When the people welcomed Jesus, they shouted "Hosanna!" Write the word "Hosanna" down the center of one side of your ribbon.** Pause for kids to write, then continue: **Now flip your ribbons over and write, "Praise and honor Jesus!"** When kids finish writing, staple the ribbons to the palm leaves. Then let kids wave their palm fronds and ribbons as you sing the following song to the tune of "Jesus Loves Me."

H-O-S-A-N-N-A (sing the letters)
Welcome Jesus every day!
Praise his power and raise his name—
Your life will never be the same!
Hosanna, hosanna!
Hosanna, hosanna!
Hosanna, hosanna!
Jesus, we love you!

Kids will love this craft idea! Make a "Welcome, Jesus!" mat to place outside your classroom door or the doorway to your church. (If you can, have kids each make a "Welcome, Jesus!" mat!) Purchase a solid-colored indoor/outdoor doormat, then embellish it using fabric paints, plastic jewels and satin cording (use tacky craft glue to attach the items). Use fabric paints to write "Welcome, Jesus!" in large letters in the center of the mat; consider writing Revelation 3:20 across the bottom of the mat. Remind kids that Jesus wants to be welcomed and invited into our lives each day!

NOT IN MY HOUSE!

The church is to be treated with respect.

Psalms 96:6; 100:4; Matthew 21:12-13; Ephesians 1:22, 23

BEFORE BEGINNING...

Before beginning, gather the Story Kit items. Tape the shower curtain to the wall and to several chairs to create a tent that will be used to represent a church or temple. Place a table outside of the tent and set the 5 plastic coins and the Picture Props on the table. This Bible story is about the time Jesus became angry at the crooked money changers outside of the temple where people could buy sacrifices to honor God. In this story lesson, kids will discover a twofold point: that it's okay to be angry at appropriate times and that God's house is to be treated with respect and honor.

Story Kit Supplies

❑ **Bible**
❑ **5 plastic coins**
❑ **plastic shower curtain**
❑ **masking tape**
❑ **Picture Props (cow, dove, sheep)**

TELLING THE STORY

Gather children next to the table by the shower-curtain tent. Ask:

★ *What does the inside of our church look like?*
★ *How do people act in and around our church? How do they treat one another? Explain.*
★ *How would you feel if people were making a mess of the church or disrespecting God in it?*

Say: **The church is a special place and was given to us by the Lord as a place where we can worship and honor God. In Jesus' day, the church was called the "temple," but it was a special place to worship God just like our church. It would make us angry if someone came along and messed up our church or treated people here badly or disrespected God, wouldn't it? It would make us very angry, and we would want to stop them because we love God and his house. That's just how Jesus felt when he saw crooked people trying to cheat others outside of God's temple long ago. Let's learn about this**

time as we retell the story. **Listen carefully to see what made Jesus so angry and to see if you agree with how Jesus felt and what he did.**

Point to the shower-curtain tent as you say: **God's house was a special place where people came to worship and praise God. Jesus went to the temple in Jerusalem to worship God, too. Jesus had just come into town in his triumphal entry, and he knew his time to teach others about God was growing short.**

Jesus went to God's house to worship God along with other people. The people could buy animals to sacrifice as gifts to God to express their love and respect. The people could buy cattle, doves, or sheep for a fair price. Hold up the pictures of the animals. **But the "money changers" who sold the animals were cheating the people and charging way too much money for them! The poorest people couldn't even afford to buy anything to give to God! Jesus saw that the money changers had tables full of money and were cheating the people at God's house! Jesus was angry! How could God's house be treated with such disrespect? What do you think Jesus did then?**

Jesus made the money changers leave at once. Jesus drove the animals out of the temple area and turned the tables of money over. Ask several children to carefully turn over the table and let the coins spill on the floor. **Then Jesus said, "My house will be called a house of prayer, but you are making it a den of robbers!" Jesus knew that God's house is a special place and should be treated with love, care, and respect! Let's clean this area and then enter his gates with thanksgiving in our hearts to honor God by learning more about respecting his house of worship.**

Have the kids set the table upright, then place the coins and Picture Props back in the Story Kit. Lead kids into the tent and sit quietly.

MAKING IT MEMORABLE

Before reading from the Bible, ask kids the following Bible-story questions.
★ *Why was Jesus so angry?*
★ *How do you think God felt about his house being treated so poorly?*

★ *Did Jesus have a right to be angry? Explain.*

Say: **There is a time to be forgiving and patient, and there is a time to be angry. Jesus was angry because of the way God's house was being treated. He wanted us to know that God's house is a place to be valued, loved, and treated with great respect. It would have made me very angry, too, to see God's house being mistreated! We want to treat God's house with love and make it a place to be close to God and others as we worship, honor, and give praise.**

Read aloud Ephesians 1:22, 23; Psalms 96:6; 100:4; 134:2; and 150:1. Then ask:

★ *Why do you think God gave us special places to meet and worship?*

★ *How does knowing that Jesus is the head of the church change your view of church?*

★ *How can we show the Lord we respect his house?*

★ *What can we do to make church a special place to worship?*

Say: **When we come into the Lord's house to worship him, we want to enter with a spirit of love and thanksgiving to express our gratitude for all he has done for us. Let's worship God now with a song in our hearts and a prayer on our lips.** Sing "I Will Enter His Courts with Thanksgiving in My Heart." Clap along joyously, then share a prayer thanking God for providing a wonderful place to worship and honor him and asking for his help in keeping your church safe, respectful, and happy.

Act out the following Scripture verse to remind kids that Jesus means for his house to be a house of prayer and respect. Then invite kids to illustrate the verse and display the pictures for everyone in church to enjoy.

"My house (use your arms to make a roof over your head)

will be called (cup hands around your mouth)

a house (make another roof over your head)

of prayer." (pretend to pray)

Mark 11:17

SERVANT JESUS

Jesus wants us to have servants' hearts.

Mark 9:35; John 13:1-14; Galatians 5:13; 1 Peter 4:10

BEFORE BEGINNING...

Before beginning, gather the Story Kit items. You'll kick off this story lesson by having kids run a lively relay geared around getting them to focus on serving others. You'll need the Story Kit at one end of the room with all of the items in it. Kids will be "serving" each other different items from the Story Kit. In this Bible-story lesson, kids will realize that no one is above serving someone else—we must all be servants of others to become more like Jesus. This story is from the Lord's Supper, when Jesus served his friends by washing their feet. The More Fun idea suggests that kids serve people in another class in a tasty way, so consider letting kids enjoy this part of the lesson!

Story Kit Supplies

❏ **Bible**
❏ **3 paper plates**
❏ **3 dish towels**
❏ **Story Kit with items**

TELLING THE STORY

Place the Story Kit at one end of the room and form three teams. Have teams line up at the end of the room opposite the Story Kit and hand the first person in each line a paper plate and dish towel. Have kids loop the dish towels over their arms "waiter-style" and hold the paper plates on their palms, in the air as if they're servers in a fine restaurant. Explain that in this serving relay, kids will balance the plates as they walk quickly to the Story Kit and choose items to put on the plates. Then kids must quickly return to the next players in line and serve them by handing over the plate and dish towel. Then those players travel to the Story Kit to pick up new items to serve, and so on. When the last person in each line has served the first player in line, have the entire team shout, "Super servers!"

After all the teams have completed the relay, have teams sit together and hold on to the dish towels. Ask:

★ *How was this serving relay like serving others we meet each day?*

★ *Why is serving others so important if we're to become more like Jesus?*

Say: **This lively relay gets us thinking about the importance of serving others. If might have seemed a bit odd serving your friends a plate of neckties or balloons or an empty pop can, but you served them anyway. Jesus' disciples had to wonder about serving, too, when Jesus served them one night by washing their feet.**

Jesus and his twelve disciples were in an upper room in a building in Jerusalem. Jesus knew this would be his last night on earth, and in a few short hours he would die for our sins on the cross. Jesus and his friends had just finished their last supper together, and Jesus wanted to teach them something very important before his time to leave would come.

Just imagine how surprised the disciples were when Jesus began washing their feet! Why would Jesus do such a thing? Well, back in Jesus' day, everyone wore sandals or went barefoot. Feet became dusty from walking along dirt roads. It was normal for people to wash their feet when going into a house. To wash someone else's feet, however, was an amazing way to serve someone in a caring way—and Jesus was God's Son! The disciples knew that they should be washing his feet instead. But Jesus wanted to teach them that even the most powerful and important people are to serve others with love and compassion. Jesus told his disciples that the greatest must be the least and that whoever wants to be master of all must be the servant of all. In other words, Jesus told us to serve others in all we do.

Jesus washed his disciples' feet, then dried them with a towel. Take your group's towel and let each person dust off a teammate's shoes. Then hand the towel to someone else in your group so they can serve, too. Pause for everyone to act out serving one another, then say: **Now let's explore more about having the heart of a servant and what that means.**

MAKING IT MEMORABLE

Invite volunteers to read aloud Mark 9:35, then ask:

★ *What did Jesus mean when he said the first must be the last?*

★ *Why is it important to be a servant of others?*

Say: **Jesus taught us in many ways, such as through his words, through his prayers, and through his actions. Throughout Jesus' entire life, he put serving God and others first in his life. Jesus served others by teaching them about God and about love and forgiveness. Jesus served by healing and helping those people in need. And Jesus served by teaching us about**

the attitudes that are important to God. One of those attitudes is the attitude of willingness to serve and to have a servant's heart. When we have a servant's heart, we're not afraid to hop in and help no matter who we're serving or how we're serving. When we have the heart of a servant, we draw closer to God!

Read aloud Deuteronomy 10:12; Galatians 5:13; and 1 Peter 4:10. Then ask:

★ *How can serving others draw us closer to God?*

★ *In what ways do we serve the Lord when we serve others?*

★ *How can you serve someone this week?*

Say: **Remember—you're never too important, too young, too old, too smart or rich or powerful not to serve others. If Jesus spent his entire life as a servant of all, we can, too! Let's share a prayer thanking Jesus for teaching us about being servants and asking him to help us have the heart of a servant.**

Share a prayer, then sing "I Have Decided to Follow Jesus" or "Serve Him" if there's time.

Offer kids an opportunity to serve in a tasty way. Provide ice cream, plastic spoons, and a variety of toppings, such as candy sprinkles, whipped cream, dried fruits, and crunchy cereal bits. Let kids prepare and serve colorful Servant Sundaes to the kids, teens, or adults in another class.

POWER OF PRAYER

Prayer is our direct line to heaven!

Luke 22:39-46; John 17:1-26; 1 Thessalonians 5:17; James 5:16

BEFORE BEGINNING...

Before beginning, gather the Story Kit items as well as the following classroom supplies: scissors. Cut six 12-inch squares from the white shelf paper. Kids will use the squares during the Bible story about Jesus' prayer in the Garden of Gethsemane. They'll assemble a cross shape from the squares and tape the pieces together using the masking tape. In this Bible-story lesson, kids will discover that even Jesus prayed and that he prayed not only for his friends and for us but also for himself!

Story Kit Supplies

❏ Bible
❏ white shelf paper
❏ masking tape

TELLING THE STORY

Seat kids in a circle on the floor near a wall of door. Set the paper squares, tape, and markers beside you. Ask:

★ *What is "prayer"?*
★ *Why do we offer prayers to God?*

Say: **Prayer is how we talk with and draw near to God. Through our prayers, we can tell God of our fears and worries, thank him for his blessings and love, and ask for what we need or what we think will help others. God promises to hear and answer every prayer we pray. Did you know that Jesus prayed, too? Jesus had quiet prayer time with God many times each day and night. He even went off by himself for entire nights to talk with God and to be close to him. Let's hear a Bible story about the night Jesus prayed a special prayer and asked God for some very important things. We'll pass paper squares around the circle as we listen to the story. When I ask a question, the person holding the paper can answer, then tape the square to the wall. As we continue, we'll be making the shape of a cross. Listen for what Jesus asked God for.** Begin passing the first paper square and telling the following story from Luke 22:39-46 and John 17:1-26.

God had a special plan when he sent Jesus to love the world. God planned for his only Son to die on the cross to forgive our sins and offer us eternal life in heaven. Stop. Do you think Jesus knew God's plan? (Pause to answer, then tape the first square to the wall or door. Pass the next paper square as you continue the story.)

Jesus knew he was to die on the cross so we would be forgiven of our sins and could be close to God again. In other words, Jesus was going to take our punishment upon himself. Stop. Do you think Jesus wanted to do this? (Pause to answer, then tape the next square to the wall or door. Pass another paper square as you continue the story.)

Jesus loved God and us so greatly that he willingly gave his life even though he knew it would be hard. Jesus loved God, and he knew that God's plan for our salvation was good and right. Stop. How does it make you feel to know that Jesus willingly gave his life for you? (Pause to answer, then tape the third square to the wall or door and pass the next paper square.)

The night before Jesus died, he prayed in a beautiful garden called Gethsemane. The garden was still and cool, and Jesus opened his heart to God in prayer. Stop. Why do you think Jesus wanted to talk to God? (Pause to answer and tape the square to the wall. Pass the next square and continue.)

Jesus wanted to talk to God because he loved God. And Jesus wanted to tell God his fears and ask for God's strength. Jesus said, "If it is possible, please do not let this happen. But if it is your will, God, I want to do whatever you ask me—whatever you think is best." Jesus asked God for strength to do what God wanted. Stop. Why did Jesus ask this of God? (Pause to answer and tape the square to the wall. Pass the next square and continue.)

Jesus prayed for himself, but he also prayed for his friends. Jesus knew his disciples would have a hard time carrying his truth to an unbelieving and mean world. Jesus asked God to watch over and strengthen his friends. Stop. Why was it awesome for Jesus to pray for his friends at a time like that? (Pause to answer the question and tape the square to the wall. Pass the next square and continue.)

Jesus prayed for himself and his friends. But he didn't stop there! Jesus also prayed for us! Jesus asked God to make us all one in him and for us to carry the truth to all people.

Jesus knew there was no other way to save people from their sins than for him to die. Jesus knew it was God's plan for our salvation. But Jesus was happy underneath it all. Why do you think Jesus was happy? Allow time for kids to share their thoughts, then continue: **Jesus was happy because he knew God heard his prayers and would answer them. And Jesus was also happy because he loves us and wants us to be with him eternally. Even Jesus prayed and asked for God's help and strength. Let's explore more about the power of prayer and why we should follow Jesus' example.**

MAKING IT MEMORABLE

Form three groups and assign each group one of the following verses to read: Matthew 21:22; 1 Thessalonians 5:17; James 5:16, . Have each group decide what is being taught about prayer, then have groups read their verses aloud and share their insights. After each group has had a turn to report its findings, ask:

★ *In what ways does prayer bring us closer to God?*

★ *Why do you think Jesus prayed so often?*

★ *In what ways does it help others when we pray for them?*

★ *How does it strengthen your faith to know that God hears and answers your prayers in his own time and way?*

Say: **Jesus knew there is great power in prayer, and that's why he prayed so often. Jesus wanted to be close to his heavenly Father, and he knew prayer was a good way to do that. When we rely on the power of prayer as Jesus did, we'll receive God's strength, peace, and direction, too! Let's end with a prayer thanking God for hearing and answering our prayers.** Share a prayer, then sing "Awesome God" if there's time.

Invite kids to decorate special prayer pillows to place on their beds to remind them to pray each night and morning. Provide each child with two 8-inch squares of craft felt and several handfuls of polyester fiberfill. Let kids use permanent markers to decorate the felt, then use tacky craft glue to glue three sides of the felt together. Stuff the pillows, then glue the fourth side.

THE SADDEST STORY

Jesus willingly died for our sins.

Matthew 27:38-66; John 10:17, 18; Romans 5:10, 11; 1 Peter 3:18

BEFORE BEGINNING...

Before beginning, gather the Story Kit items as well as the following classroom supplies: scissors for each child. Cut shelf paper into 4-by-12-inch rectangles. Cut one rectangle for each child plus several extras. Practice folding and snipping the paper according to the story directions so you become familiar with how this cut-n-tell story should go. You'll be leading kids in cutting and folding along with the story of Jesus' death on the cross, so be sure you have a pair of scissors for each child. (The next story lesson is the resurrection story.) In this story lesson, kids will discover that Jesus willingly gave up his life for us for two main reasons: because it was God's plan, and because he loved us so greatly.

Story Kit Supplies

❑ **Bible**
❑ **white shelf paper**

TELLING THE STORY

Gather kids in a circle and distribute the paper rectangles and scissors. Ask kids to tell about the saddest thing they have ever heard about or know. Then say: **Sad stories might be tough to hear, but they really can get us thinking and feeling. Today's Bible story is the saddest story we can imagine. But it's a story that encourages us to really think, feel, and understand just what Jesus has done for us and how much he loves God and us. We'll use paper rectangles and scissors to tell this story, so listen and watch carefully—and do what I do.**

Lead kids in folding and cutting their papers as you unfold the story of Jesus' death on the cross. Go slowly enough so all kids can keep up. You may want to let kids sit with partners so they can help each other if needed.

Say: **God sent Jesus into the world to love people, to serve them, and to teach them about our Father in heaven. But God had an even bigger plan**

when he sent Jesus to live among us. Jesus was sent into the world to take the punishment for our sins and to offer us a way to eternal life with God. (Fold the paper in half, then fold down the right top corner to make a point that points upward to heaven.)

Jesus and his disciples had shared their last supper, and Jesus had prayed in the garden as he waited for God's plan to be fulfilled. Just before sunrise, Jesus was arrested and brought to Pontius Pilate's house. He was the mean Roman governor who would put Jesus on trial for claiming to be God's Son. (Fold the other corner down so the paper now looks like a house.) **Pontius Pilate didn't love God, and he didn't like Jesus claiming to be king. Pontius Pilate couldn't decide what to do with Jesus, so he asked the people in the crowds if they wanted Jesus or a robber who had been arrested to be set free. What do you think the people said?** Pause for answers. **The people wanted Jesus to be hung on the cross, so they let the robber go free.**

The door was opened, and Jesus stepped outside. (Fold the left side of the house over the right side.) **They had to cut through the crowds on their way to Golgotha, the place where Jesus was to be crucified.** (Cut up the center of the paper shape. Open the shapes and pick out the two long rectangles. Hold them up.) **Jesus had been whipped and beaten by the soldiers. Oh, how it hurt Jesus—but not as much as how the people felt about him. And not as much as when the Roman soldiers threw dice to see who would get Jesus' robe!** (Open up the two small squares and hold them up.)

Then Jesus was hung on the cross to die in a slow, awful way. (Open up the cross and hold it up.) **Jesus was God's powerful and divine Son, and he could have zapped himself away from the cross and the pain and anguish—but yet he willingly chose to die for us! Why? Because Jesus loved God and wanted to fulfill God's plan for our salvation. And because Jesus loved us so greatly and wanted us to be forgiven and given the chance for eternal life!** (Hold the cross to your heart.) **Because of Jesus' great love, he suffered on the cross ... willingly and freely.**

Offer a prayer thanking Jesus for his love and for dying for our sins so we can be forgiven and enjoy eternal life. Then say: **Let's read more about why Jesus chose to die for us and how his love could be so great.**

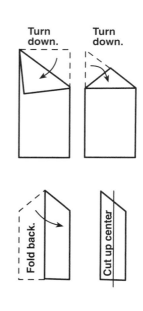

Turn down.　Turn down.

Fold back.　Cut up center

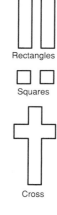

Rectangles

Squares

Cross

MAKING IT MEMORABLE

Read aloud John 10:17, 18; 1 Corinthians 15:3, 4; 1 Peter 3:18; and Romans 5:10, 11. Then ask:

★ *Why was this the saddest story in the Bible?*
★ *Why was Jesus' willingness to die for us a miraculous show of his love?*
★ *In what way was Jesus' death on the cross part of God's plan for us?*
★ *How do you feel knowing Jesus died for you?*
★ *How can you thank Jesus for taking our punishment?*

Say: **We can all imagine someone being willing to giving up a seat on a crowded bus so another person might sit down or even giving up a week's allowance to donate to a food bank. But it is so hard to imagine someone with love great enough to willingly die for people who were filled with hate, envy, and evil—and yet Jesus did this. Jesus willingly gave up his life and took our punishment so that we could be forgiven of our sins and have eternal life with our Father in heaven.** End by singing "'Tis So Sweet to Trust in Jesus," then challenge kids to present this cut-n-tell Bible story to their families and friends.

Let older children make unusual crosses to remind them that Jesus willingly died for us all. Before class, file the ends of 4-inch nails to make them dull. Then hand each child a pair of nails and an 8-inch piece of thin wire. Let kids work in pairs to wind wire around the centers of the nails to make crosses. Then twist on a 20-inch loop of wire to make the crosses into necklaces.

ALIVE FOREVER!

Jesus defeated death and is alive forevermore!

Mark 16:6; Luke 24:1-12; Romans 8:34

BEFORE BEGINNING...

Story Kit Supplies

❏ Bible
❏ 2 lunch sacks
❏ ball
❏ Picture Props (woman, angel, Jesus)

Before beginning, gather the Story Kit items as well as the following classroom supplies: scissors and clear tape. Prepare the lunch sack with a secret flap as follows. Cut the side panel from one of the lunch sacks and tape it to the inside of the other sack at the bottom so it creates a flap. When the flap is held against the side of the bag, the bag should appear to be whole and normal. During the Bible story of Jesus' resurrection, you'll place the picture of Jesus into the flap. (The kids will think you just dropped the picture into the main portion of the bag, since the flap is secret!) You'll roll the ball in front of the sack, then at the appointed time, a volunteer will roll away the ball, and you will quickly hold the flap against the side of the bag (to trap the picture inside) and hold up the bag so kids can see that it's now empty! In this Bible-story lesson, kids will learn that Jesus had the ultimate victory over death and that he is alive and promises to be with us forever.

TELLING THE STORY

Be sure you have the sack with the secret flap. (Don't let the kids see the flap. Hold it against the side of the bag at all times.) Place the Picture Props and ball beside you. Seat kids in a group in front of you and ask:

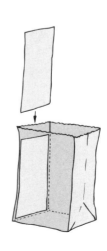

★ *Would you like to live forever?*
★ *Who would you live with if you could live forever?*

Say: **The Bible tells about a promise of "forever" life, of having eternal life with our heavenly Father. Last week you heard the saddest story ever, but it**

didn't end with sadness; it ended with the most joyous ending there could be! Let's listen to this amazing story of a miraculous victory over death and the glorious life we are promised.

Hold up the picture of Jesus and say: **When Jesus died on the cross for our sins, the people put him in a cavelike tomb.** Place the picture of Jesus in the secret flap of the bag, but make it appear as if you placed the picture in the regular part of the sack. (Remember to keep holding the flap against the side of the bag.) Set the bag on the floor. **Then to make sure no one disturbed the tomb, a large, heavy stone was rolled in front of the tomb.** Ask a volunteer to place the ball in front of the sack opening. **Jesus' friends were so sad and discouraged. They went home to pray and share their sadness. And for three long, dark days, the friends waited. Close your eyes for a moment and think of what it must have been like during those sad days. "Jesus is gone," thought his friends. "We'll never see him again." The disciples were so sad.**

But then the third day dawned bright and still. Mary and her friend decided to go to the tomb. Set the picture of the woman beside the tomb. **They were still very sad and thought that nothing could be bright or happy again. Then what do you think they saw when they arrived at the tomb? The stone had been rolled away from the tomb, and there was an angel!** Hold up the picture of the angel, then place it beside the sack. **The angel was so bright that the women were afraid! Then the angel spoke to them. "Who are you looking for? Jesus is not here," said the angel. "Jesus is alive!" Mary and her friend couldn't believe it! Jesus was in the tomb, wasn't he? They peeked inside. What did they see? Let's look!** Invite a volunteer to roll the ball away from the sack "tomb." Let kids peek inside the empty sack. Then say: **Jesus wasn't there! Jesus had overcome death and was alive! Mary and her friend were filled with amazement and joy and ran to tell their friends that Jesus was alive, just as God's plan promised. And Jesus is alive today, too. Those who love Jesus and accept him will never die but have forever life with God! Isn't that wonderful? And that's the happiest story in the Bible—or anywhere!**

MAKING IT MEMORABLE

Read aloud Mark 16:6 and 1 Corinthians 15:56, 57. Ask

★ *Why do you think God's plan was for us to have eternal life through Jesus?*

★ *How does it feel knowing that Jesus is alive and with us right now?*

★ *How do you feel knowing you can live forever with Jesus?*

Say: **We know and celebrate the fact that Jesus is alive and with us always. But what is he doing now, and what promise has he made us?** Read aloud Romans 8:34; John 14:2; and Matthew 28:20b. Then ask:

★ *In what ways is Jesus still helping us all the time?*

★ *How does it feel to know that Jesus is preparing a place for us in heaven?*

★ *What promise did Jesus make about being with us?*

★ *How does it help strengthen your faith to know that Jesus will be with you forever?*

★ *Why is it important to tell others about the chance for eternal life with Jesus?*

Say: **Jesus had the ultimate victory over death and is alive and with us all the time. What a celebration every day to know that Jesus is with us all the way!** End by singing "Christ the Lord Is Risen Today" or "Alive Forevermore!"

Let kids make their own secret sacks using lunch sacks. Have them color the sacks brown, using markers or crayons to look more like stone or rock. Then let kids draw the figure of Jesus on index cards or photocopy the Picture Prop picture of Jesus from page 110 to use in their secret sacks. (You may also wish to copy the pictures of Mary and the angel for kids.) Let kids practice telling this Bible story with partners, then challenge them to present this story at home to their families as they remind others that Jesus is alive and promises to be with us forevermore.

GOOD NEWS!

It's important to tell others about Jesus.

Matthew 28:16-20; 1 Thessalonians 2:8; Colossians 1:3-6

BEFORE BEGINNING...

Before beginning, gather the Story Kit items. In this lively Bible story of Jesus' ascension and Great Commission to tell others about him, kids will be holding the shower curtain and tossing in Story Kit items that represent reasons we want to tell others about Jesus and the truth he brings us. Kids will discover there are many reasons to tell others about Jesus and learn how we can meet the challenge of the Great Commission.

Story Kit Supplies

- ❏ Bible
- ❏ plastic shower curtain
- ❏ masking tape
- ❏ ball
- ❏ large jingle bell
- ❏ 1 plastic coin
- ❏ ball of string

TELLING THE STORY

Spread the plastic shower curtain on the floor and have kids sit around the edges of it. Place the Story Kit items beside you. Ask:

★ *When have you had an important message to share with someone?*
★ *How did you tell your message?*
★ *What if you hadn't told that important message?*

Say: **Some messages are very important and are made to be shared with others because we know these messages will help people. If we forget to tell those important messages, someone may be hurt or left out. In our Bible story today, Jesus the most important message of all, and he wanted that message told. You can help tell the story. As the story unfolds, we'll toss items up and down in the shower curtain to show how important messages can bounce from one person to another.**

Have kids stand around the edge of the shower curtain and hold the edges in their hands. Have kids lift the shower curtain up and down in rhythm as you say: **Jesus had been raised from death, and his friends were joyous to know he was alive. Jesus told his friends to follow him, and he led them to the base of a mountain. Then something amazing happened! Jesus**

107

began to rise into the air! But before Jesus was lifted to heaven, he told his friends a very important message.

Jesus told them to go into the whole world and to tell people about his love. (Toss the ball onto the shower curtain and bounce it up and down as you continue.) Since this ball is round, it will remind us that Jesus' message said to go to all places throughout the world and to teach others about Jesus' love, forgiveness, and gift of eternal life. This was the first part of Jesus' message. What was next?

Toss in the roll of masking tape and bounce it along with the ball. Say: Tape is sticky and reminds us that we want to stick close to God, Jesus, and the Holy Spirit. In his important message, Jesus told his disciples to baptize people in the name of the Father, Son, and Holy Spirit. In this way, we accept Jesus into our lives and tell him we want to follow and obey him. This was the next part of Jesus' message. What was next?

Toss in the ball of string and bounce it along with the ball and masking tape. Say: String ties things together, and this remind us of how Jesus' teaching is tied to obeying God. Jesus told his disciples to teach people of the importance of obeying God. He wanted us to help others learn God's truths and how they are tied to our salvation, forgiveness, love, and eternal life through Jesus. This was the third part of Jesus' message. What was next?

Toss in the jingle bell and say: Jingle bells are used in songs and celebrations and remind us that we can celebrate the fact that Jesus is alive and promises to be with us forever. Jesus wanted us to know that he will always be with us throughout eternity. So Jesus had four important points in his message: to go into all the world to tell others about him; to baptize others in the name of the Father, Son, and Holy Spirit; to teach others to obey God; and to trust the promise of his continual presence in our lives. And what does that all add up to? Toss in the plastic coin and say: It adds up to the greatest treasure and most valuable message we can share with other people!

Stop bouncing the items and carefully set the shower curtain flat on the floor, leaving the Story Kit items in the center. You'll use the items later.

MAKING IT MEMORABLE

Read Matthew 28:19, 20; 1 Thessalonians 2:8; and Colossians 1:5-6. Then ask:
★ *Why is Jesus' message so important for us? for others who may not yet know Jesus?*
★ *Why do you think Jesus wants us to take the Good News all over the world?*
★ *In what ways does it help others to hear the Good news about Jesus?*
★ *How can you tell someone about Jesus?*

★ *Who is one person you can tell Jesus' important message to this week?*

Say: **There are so many messages floating around each day in our lives. Phone messages, messages in the mail, articles in the newspapers, and messages on e-mail. But none of these messages has the power or purpose that Jesus' message to us has! When we go into all the world to share the truth about Jesus and his message of salvation with others, it's the most important message they will ever receive! Let's share a prayer asking for Jesus' help in conveying his message to other people throughout our lives.**

Share a prayer, then gather kids around the edges of the shower curtain again. End by singing "Go Tell It on the Mountain" as you bounce the Story Kit items joyously in time to the music.

Play Message Ball using the ball from the Story Kit. Form a circle, squiggly line, or other shape. Then begin tossing the ball down the line or around the circle as kids each call out the first names of people they can tell about Jesus. Encourage kids to think of friends, family members, kids at school, neighbors, and community workers. Set a time limit of five minutes and challenge kids to keep naming names and tossing the ball until "time's up!" Then remind kids that there's never enough time to tell others about the Good News of Jesus!

PICTURE PROPS

Angel

Jesus

PICTURE PROPS

PICTURE PROPS

VERSE CARDS FOR TALL LOVE

"A new command I give you: Love one another. As I have loved you, so you must love one another."
John 13:34

"Therefore, if anyone is in Christ, he is a new creation; the old has gone, the new has come!"
2 Corinthians 5:17

"Be kind and compassionate to one another, forgiving each other, just as in Christ God forgave you."
Ephesians 4:32